T0334201

Cambridge Elements ≡

Elements in Shakespeare and Pedagogy
edited by
Liam E. Semler
University of Sydney
Gillian Woods
Birkbeck College, University of London

READING SHAKESPEARE THROUGH DRAMA

Jane Coles
UCL Institute of Education

Maggie Pitfield
Goldsmiths, University of London

CAMBRIDGE
UNIVERSITY PRESS

CAMBRIDGE
UNIVERSITY PRESS

University Printing House, Cambridge CB2 8BS, United Kingdom

One Liberty Plaza, 20th Floor, New York, NY 10006, USA

477 Williamstown Road, Port Melbourne, VIC 3207, Australia

314–321, 3rd Floor, Plot 3, Splendor Forum, Jasola District Centre,
New Delhi – 110025, India

103 Penang Road, #05–06/07, Visioncrest Commercial, Singapore 238467

Cambridge University Press is part of the University of Cambridge.

It furthers the University's mission by disseminating knowledge in the pursuit of
education, learning, and research at the highest international levels of excellence.

www.cambridge.org
Information on this title: www.cambridge.org/9781009001984
DOI: 10.1017/9781009004268

© Jane Coles and Maggie Pitfield 2022

First published 2022

A catalogue record for this publication is available from the British Library.

ISBN 978-1-009-00198-4 Paperback
ISSN 2632-816X (online)
ISSN 2632-8151 (print)

Reading Shakespeare through Drama

Elements in Shakespeare and Pedagogy

DOI: 10.1017/9781009004268

First published online: June 2022

Jane Coles

UCL Institute of Education

Maggie Pitfield

Goldsmiths, University of London

Author for correspondence: Jane Coles, j.coles@ucl.ac.uk

ABSTRACT: *Reading Shakespeare through Drama* arises out of case study research which focuses on reading as a sociocultural practice. Underpinned by theories of reading, learning, drama and play, it is nevertheless rooted in the everyday work of secondary English classrooms. Utilising the dialogic ambiguities inherent in Shakespeare's play scripts, this collaborative approach to reading pays particular attention to adolescent readers as meaning-makers and cultural producers. The authors examine different iterations of 'active Shakespeare' pedagogies in the UK, the USA and Australia, drawing a distinction between 'reading through drama' as an approach and the theatre-inflected practices promoted by well-known arts-based institutions. Observational and interview data highlight the importance of addressing issues concerning identity and representation that are inevitably raised by the study of canonical literature. Importantly, this Element situates teachers' practice within broader ideological contexts at the institutional and national policy levels, particularly from the perspective of England's highly regulated system of schooling.

KEYWORDS: active Shakespeare, secondary English, reading, educational drama, sociocultural practice

ISBNs: 9781009001984 (PB), 9781009004268 (OC)

ISSNs: 2632-816X (online), 2632-8151 (print)

Contents

1 Introduction 1

2 Frameworks: Learning, Reading and Playing 9

3 Shakespeare in Practice: Institutional Constraints and Teacher Agency 32

4 Shakespeare in Practice: Reading through Drama 53

5 Conclusions 77

References 86

1 Introduction

Our central aim in this Element is to explore the capacity of drama to activate productive, reader-focused engagement when studying a Shakespeare play in a school classroom. We make no claims to originality in suggesting that drama might profitably be used to teach Shakespeare. What distinguishes our approach from other publications about 'active Shakespeare', however, is our particular focus on reading as a sociocultural practice rather than on drama methods per se. The specific type of learner-centred educational drama we have in mind overlaps with and is supportive of classroom reading practices in complex, dynamic ways. In Section 2 we define what we mean by 'reading through drama', bringing together theories of reading, learning, drama and play. In subsequent sections we apply the concept to real-world examples of classroom interaction using observational data, video recordings of secondary school English lessons and interviews with learners and their teachers. What does 'reading Shakespeare through drama' look like in practice? What are the potential benefits of working in this way, and what are the challenges? While we are mindful that the case studies which provide the empirical data for this Element are situated historically and culturally in specific London classrooms, our belief is that they raise pedagogical questions which will be of interest to teachers of Shakespeare in a far wider range of contexts.

Background: 'The Autobiography of the Question'

In explaining the background to our research, we adopt Jane Miller's (1995) methodological invitation to explore 'the autobiography of the question', to situate ourselves personally and historically in the complex network of social relations that constitute school classrooms.[1] Consequently we do not pretend to be disinterested, objective observers when offering our analyses of classroom interactions. The assumption we make is that our

---

[1] Miller (1995) argues that 'the autobiography of the question' not only presents a way of 'historicizing the questions [researchers] are addressing', but also offers a 'sense of working consciously within and against accepted [academic] forms' (p. 26).

own professional and ideological biographies have served to shape the values and beliefs we bring to our work as educators and researchers and these therefore inflect the ways in which we perceive meaning-making practices in classrooms (Doecke, 2015). We (Jane and Maggie) share similar histories of teaching in multi-ethnic, socially mixed London classrooms during the 1980s and 1990s. Our teaching careers span politically turbulent moments in terms of late twentieth-century educational reform in the UK, including the introduction of compulsory Shakespeare in the first National Curriculum (NC) for English (1989) and subsequent – highly contested – assessment impositions. Part of the impetus for this Element arises out of ongoing professional and political conversations that have sustained us both across our long careers in education, including a period of five years when we taught together in the same secondary school English department, and much later when we worked together for a similar period of time in the same university education department.

Our specific interest in the teaching of Shakespeare was originally prompted by a number of pivotal events in the late 1980s: our growing unease with the nationalistic discourses generated by Margaret Thatcher's Conservative government (1979–90), particularly from our perspective as teachers working in multi-ethnic urban school environments; the imposition of statutory Shakespeare as part of a new NC (which we say more about later in this section); the launch of Rex Gibson's national Shakespeare in Schools Project (one of us, Jane, was seconded to the Project in 1987); and the publication of Jonathan Dollimore and Alan Sinfield's groundbreaking *Political Shakespeare* in 1985. Whereas Gibson's project attempted to shake up conventional teaching methods (which we discuss in more detail in Section 2), in effect Dollimore and Sinfield's (1985) unashamedly ideological form of critical practice ripped up the old 'lit crit' certainties that underpinned conventional ways of reading and interpreting Shakespeare. Assessing the thirty-year legacy of *Political Shakespeare*, Graham Holderness (one of the contributors) claims that it has 'irrevocably altered the academic landscape of Shakespeare Studies' (2014, p. 5). It profoundly influenced our thinking at the time, although it posed a challenge to those of us working within the heavily regulated practices of secondary English classrooms. Both of us chose to explore these tensions and possibilities further, albeit in different ways, for our respective master's dissertations completed part-time at separate points in the early 1990s.

Since then our specialist research and publication interests have diverged, but in complementary ways. 'Reading through drama' as a concept was first developed by Maggie (Pitfield, 2020), who comes to our current project from the direction of research into educational drama, specifically how drama is employed as part of the reading process in the secondary English classroom. Jane's area of research has largely remained focused on the teaching and assessing of Shakespeare, in particular the competing ways in which Shakespeare as a cultural and literary phenomenon has been constructed by and within the school system.

Of enduring significance to us both, and of direct relevance to our current approach to teaching Shakespeare, is our very deeply held commitment to a comprehensive (non-selective) system of schooling which caters for the needs and interests of all learners. In our teaching careers and latterly in our university-based work with postgraduate trainee and experienced English teachers, we have continued to develop an inclusive pedagogy that is attentive to the social and cultural lives of students and that regards classrooms as social, dialogic spaces where meanings are made rather than merely transmitted. These principles have increasingly positioned us at odds with the direction of educational reform introduced by successive governments in the UK since the 1990s. Indeed, when Brenton Doecke and Douglas McClenaghan (2011) describe schooling in Australia as progressively marked by curricular imposition, standardised testing and constricting accountability procedures, they could just as easily be describing current educational systems in Britain and the USA. But Doecke and McClenaghan remind us that the relationship between teachers, their students and the system of schooling in which they find themselves is both complex and often contradictory. It is crucial to recognise that even in unpromising circumstances, teachers (and their students) time and time again exhibit agency and that schools remain sites of cultural production and contestation. So, while in Section 3 we consider the very real ways in which secondary English teachers may come to feel pedagogically constrained by working in highly regulated, outcomes-focused environments, in Section 4 we provide countervailing evidence of teachers and students prising open productive spaces within which they engage collectively with Shakespeare, and we explore the conditions and teacher dispositions that might have enabled these different ways of working.

First, however, we contextualise our examples of classroom practice by examining versions of curricular Shakespeare produced by British policy-makers over the past thirty years.

Shakespeare in the British National Curriculum (1989–Present)

In his analysis of neoliberalism, David Harvey (2005) notes how successive governments in the UK and the USA from the 1980s onwards have mobilised traditional forms of culture in an attempt to disguise the inevitable social fragmentation wrought by increased marketisation. British politicians' obsession with Shakespeare has had a long and colonially tainted history (see, e.g., Trivedi, 2011), but it reached fresh levels of fervour towards the end of the past century and has enjoyed something of a resurgence in the past decade. In the late 1980s alarmist discourses about the dilution of national identity and falling literacy standards formed the mood music against which the first NC in England and Wales was formulated in 1989.[2] As a key part of what Stephen Ball (1993, p. 195) characterises as an ideological project of 'cultural restoration', the Conservative government privileged English within the whole NC as a designated 'core' subject and by statute installed Shakespeare and Standard English at its heart. Although the original government-appointed subject working group for English, the Cox Committee, resisted strong political pressure to prescribe a list of canonical 'set texts' (see Cox, 1991), they were happy to enforce Shakespeare as the sole representative of the canon, justifying the move with references to 'universal truths' and

---

[2] At the time NC legislation applied to England and Wales. In 1998 Wales along with Scotland and Northern Ireland gained further devolved powers, including greater autonomy over education policy. In choosing the appropriate national descriptor, we follow Jones (2016) by using England (or England and Wales where relevant) in reference to specific aspects of education policy authorised by the national government in Westminster, but Britain (or UK) when referring to broader, more general political/cultural issues.

'language [which] expresses rich and subtle meanings beyond that of any other English writer' (DES/Welsh Office, 1989, paragraph 7.16). In the intervening thirty years the NC for English has undergone four further government-authorised revisions throughout which Shakespeare has retained his prominence. Regardless of the particular political party in office, each curricular iteration makes explicit reference to Shakespeare's central place within the 'English literary heritage', consistently constructing his plays as *literary* texts to be taught within the Programme of Study for Reading at both Key Stage 3 (KS3 11–14 years) and Key Stage 4 (KS4 14–16 years). The most recent version (DfE, 2014), couched in explicitly Arnoldian terms of cultural elitism (Coles, 2013; Elliott, 2014), actually increases the number of Shakespeare plays to be consumed across the five years of secondary schooling (from two to three). Any sense that young readers might take an active role in making meaning out of their textual encounters is all but eliminated by policymakers' deathly instruction that students should be 'taught' to 'appreciate' the English literary canon (DfE, 2014). This directive encapsulates the narrow, unambitious nature of the reading aims for the whole of KS4. Nowhere is it suggested that the point of this literary education might be to encourage students to enjoy reading for its own sake, or that students should interrogate and interpret Shakespeare and other literary works or, indeed, become producers of literary texts themselves.

Political decisions about curriculum content are always likely to be contested, particularly when they legitimise specific types of cultural knowledge and specific ways in which readers are represented (Coles, 2020); indeed, right from the moment of inception the NC for English has provoked critical debate (e.g., Jones, 1992). What triggered outright rebellion, however, was the accompanying framework of assessment which formed a cornerstone of Conservative education reforms. Perhaps the most controversial aspect was the launch of KS3 national Standard Attainment Tests (SATs) for fourteen-year-olds as part of the 1993 curriculum revision (DfE, 1993), designed in effect to ensure professional compliance with specified curriculum requirements.[3] In addition, SAT

---

[3] The SATs applied to designated 'core' subjects: English, maths and science.

results were to be used as a performance measure, setting school against school in competitive league tables. The whole initiative was met by implacable professional resistance spearheaded by English teachers who were, in part, objecting to the misappropriation of Shakespeare as the main subject of one of these tests. The reductive style of questioning in the Shakespeare test was perfectly satirised by a contemporary cartoon in the *Times Educational Supplement* which portrayed a fretful pupil poring over an exam desk confronted by a manic robot demanding, 'Why did Romeo fall in love with Juliet? GIVE THREE REASONS!' (cited in Coles, 1994, p. 27). The national anti-SATs campaign, in which we were both actively involved as trade unionists and English specialists, brought together an unprecedented coalition of teaching unions, subject associations and parents' groups. Although the ensuing boycott of the tests in 1993 successfully forced a government retreat, KS3 SATs were resumed in modified form in 1995 and remained in place until 2008, despite continuing criticism by English teachers and their main subject association, the National Association for the Teaching of English (NATE).[4]

Over time the Shakespeare test requirements evolved into a formulaic 'lit crit' essay question on a set play, covering one of four possible areas of focus: character; ideas, themes and issues; the language of the text; and the text in performance (QCA, 2002). Teachers were expected to focus their students' attention on certain key scenes identified in advance by the government's examination authority (in Section 4 we include data collected from a Year 9 class operating under this tightly prescribed system). The published mark schemes made clear that, whatever the precise test question,

---

[4] Rex Gibson, founder of the national Shakespeare in Schools Project (see Section 2), argued passionately against the 'trivialising experience of reducing Shakespeare's imagination and intellectual richness to a 30 minute written test' (Gibson, 1993, p. 79). In a survey he conducted of more than six hundred English teachers, 92 per cent expressed concern about the Shakespeare SATs. Periodic surveys carried out by subject associations and teachers' unions indicated a persistently similar level of discontent (e.g., ATL, ATM and NATE, 1998); also see NATE position statements in various issues of *NATE News* – for example, Summer 1993, Summer 1995, September 2004.

successful answers required memorisation of key quotations and commentary on language features, even if the question ostensibly focused on 'the text in performance' (Coles, 2003). Consequently managerially expedient decisions in some schools resulted in specialist drama departments being co-opted into servicing the SATs apparatus by taking responsibility for performance aspects of the set Shakespeare play with Year 9 classes (Pitfield, 2006). The resulting artificial separation of Shakespeare in performance from other forms of interpretation represented the antithesis of the 'active Shakespeare' movement (discussed in more detail in Section 2) and threatened to turn the clock back in terms of literary critical approaches.[5]

Changes to assessment regimes at the end of KS4, although at times controversial, have been less explosively contentious in comparison with those at KS3 (perhaps because some kind of national examination system has marked the end of compulsory schooling throughout the post-war period). Remodified certification for sixteen-year-olds introduced in 1986 (the General Certificate of Secondary Education or GCSE) offered coursework options in most subjects, including English. Assessing Shakespeare through teacher-assessed, externally moderated coursework was extremely popular with English teachers, offering a degree of professional autonomy and pedagogical flexibility. For a short period of time, teachers could even opt to assess students' response to Shakespeare orally. However, with each NC revision over the past thirty years, teacher-controlled elements of assessment have been steadily eroded by government edict, eventually eradicated completely by the Conservative-led coalition government in 2014. At the time of writing, Shakespeare at GCSE is assessed solely by means of terminal written examination, whereas at the time of the research we describe in Sections 3 and 4, Year 10 and Year 11 classes (KS4) were still enjoying the relative freedom offered by Shakespeare coursework.

The Research

The school-based evidence cited in Sections 3 and 4 is drawn from two separate but complementary case studies we conducted sequentially

---

[5] There is evidence that this situation did not significantly change even following the government's abandonment of the tests in 2008 (Pitfield, 2013).

between 2006 and 2016. This period encompasses national assessment of Shakespeare by terminal exam (KS3 SATs) and through residual forms of coursework (GCSE). While there are differences in the precise research focus of each case study, a common feature is the close attention paid to the teaching of Shakespeare in everyday secondary school classrooms. For the purposes of this current project, we have selected 'significant moments' (Yandell, 2016, p. 64) from this wider data set, as far as the limited space of this Element will allow. Analysis of these moments (taken from transcripts of videoed lessons, recorded interviews conducted with teachers and with focus groups of students) exemplifies our arguments about Shakespeare pedagogy and reading practices.

This type of qualitative research, which borrows from ethnographic approaches, consciously blurs the lines between 'insider'/'outsider' researcher positions (Swain, 2006). Countering those who would question the validity of such research, such as Sarah Olive (2015), we seek to reassert the value of fine-grained, qualitative investigations that are attentive to classrooms as socially and culturally complex sites. It is important to note that our research was not set up as a scientifically measurable intervention. On the contrary, our interest lies in *processes* rather than outcomes. Based on our own experiences over many years of live classroom observations and subsequent, repeated viewing of video footage, like Doecke (2015) and John Yandell (2016) we have become increasingly interested in meanings that are made in small, salient moments of learner interaction. Our professional closeness to these classroom environments not only increases our sensitivity as readers of the research data, but also enhances our awareness of the ways in which both teachers and students are differentially situated. From an ethical perspective a heightening of our understanding of the local contexts increases our respect for the participants. We make no claims as to the generalisability of our case study findings; rather, we draw attention to the particularities of local circumstances (Yandell, 2019). By asking specific questions we seek to offer analytical insights into the processes involved in reading a Shakespeare play in these classrooms, insights that we hope readers may find of relevance in considering other contexts with which they are familiar.

The Schools and the Teachers

Our four case study schools are all secondary comprehensives based in London with which we have a professional familiarity. For ethical reasons, names of schools, teachers and students have been appropriately anonymised throughout. Permissions were sought and consent obtained from all participants in accordance with British Educational Research Association (BERA) ethical guidelines current at the time of conducting the research. These are the schools and teachers who are referenced in later sections:

- Eastgate (mixed gender) – Marie (Year 9: *Macbeth*. Data collected in 2006 covering preparation for externally assessed written SATs examination); Beth (Year 10: *Henry V*. Data collected in 2009 when Shakespeare was assessed by coursework essay).
- Parkside (mixed gender) – Pip (Year 10: *Romeo and Juliet*. Data collected in 2008 when Shakespeare was assessed by coursework essay).
- Downham Fields (mixed gender) – interviews with Paul, Chloe, Emmanuel, Claire and Jamie undertaken throughout the academic year 2009/10 following the abandonment of SATs.
- Woodside (boys) – Shona (Year 7 class: *A Midsummer Night's Dream*. Data collected across the academic year 2011/12).
- Interviews with Woodside students conducted in 2012 and again with the same students shortly prior to their GCSE examinations in 2016, the final year in which an element of coursework was allowed (albeit highly constrained, time-limited and written under 'controlled' classroom conditions).

Each of the schools is socially and ethnically mixed, reflecting the diverse populations that make up many areas of London. For the purposes of our current enquiry, we have selected relevant examples from a larger data set of teachers and classes, and these form the basis of our analysis in Sections 3 and 4.

2 Frameworks: Learning, Reading and Playing

Any exploration of classroom pedagogy must inevitably draw attention to what is meant by 'learning' and should consequently raise questions about the nature of disciplinary knowledge as produced within curricular systems.

Both issues become more pressing when the subject of enquiry concerns a body of canonical texts prescribed by politicians for compulsory study in schools. Current debates around 'powerful knowledge' (e.g., Young, 2008) and the 'knowledge-rich curriculum' (e.g., Gibb, 2017) have been prompted in part by the work of US educationalist E. D. Hirsch (1987, 2007), who proposes what amounts to an inverted form of Bourdieusian cultural capital. According to Hirsch, there exist universally agreed sets of canonical knowledge, acquaintance with which all young people are entitled in the name of empowerment and social justice. Nick Gibb, British Schools Minister and self-confessed Hirsch enthusiast (see Gibb, 2017), expresses his version of this educational philosophy thus:

> Education is about the transfer of knowledge from one generation to the next ... The rich language of Shakespeare should be the common property of us all. The great figures of literature that still populate the conversations of all those who regard themselves as well-educated should be known to all ... And they must be taught to everyone.
>
> (Gibb, 2010)

Knowledge is conceived of as reified, stable and self-explanatory, a commodity that can be exchanged in a straightforward, one-way classroom transaction between the knowledgeable and the knowledge-less. We think it is important to explain in some detail why we unequivocally reject this monologic transmission model of teaching and learning and why, when it comes to Shakespeare in particular, we believe the development of literary knowledge involves a much more complex process of engagement than is implied by Hirsch or current policymakers in Britain.[6]

---

[6] As from September 2021 Gibb's concept of 'cultural capital' is officially enshrined in the government's school inspection framework: 'As part of making the judgement about the quality of education, inspectors will consider the extent to which schools are equipping pupils with the knowledge and cultural capital they need to succeed in life'. See www.gov.uk/government/publications/school-inspection-handbook-eif/school-inspection-handbook.

Theories of Learning and Play

Foundational to our analyses of classroom practices are the social construc-tivist theories of Soviet psychologist Lev Vygotsky, whose early twentieth-century writings have been influential in Western educational thinking since they were first translated into English in the 1970s. Vygotsky proposes that all learning arises out of sociocultural processes and contexts. He particu-larly focuses on the twin function of language as both a social and a psychological tool (1986), arguing that we use language not only to communicate existing knowledge and experiences to others, but also to develop new knowledge and (re)organise our individual thoughts. According to Vygotsky these functions do not operate independently of each other. Children's early language development is shaped by the parti-cular community they are born into; as they go on to encounter fresh experiences and new contexts, they are naturally engaged in an internal psychological process of adaptation and reinterpretation: 'In that process, the relation of thought to word undergoes changes that themselves may be regarded as development in the functional sense' (p. 218). In other words, there is an ongoing dialectical relationship between learners' cognitive development and their sociocultural and material environment, both within and outside school.

Clearly this insight has relevance to our understanding of knowledge acquisition and the teaching of curriculum content in schools. Vygotsky argues that 'direct teaching of concepts' alone – similar to Gibb's 'transmis-sion model' of teaching – merely leads to 'parrotlike repetition' and 'empty verbalism' (1986, p. 150) on the part of the learners. Indeed, Vygotsky proposes a reconceptualisation of learning and knowledge acquisition. He states that the development of 'mature concepts' relies upon a dynamic interplay between the abstract, disciplinary knowledge taught in school (what Vygotsky calls 'scientific concepts') and learners' existing, everyday knowledge accumulated from real life experiences ('spontaneous concepts'). Vygotsky regards this as a two-directional interaction with spontaneous concepts becoming more systematised and abstract as they connect with scientific concepts, which in turn take on a more concrete form as they interact with a learner's store of everyday knowledge. Thus, as more recent commentators have suggested, 'there is a very real sense in which education cannot be reduced to the acquisition of a body of information' (Daniels, 1996, p. 11). Yandell (2016, p. 16) takes this a step further, pointing out that Vygotsky's ideas about concept formation have the potential to represent a significant shift in pedagogical orientation:

> To suggest that there is a dialectical relationship between everyday and scientific concepts, however, is to make a further claim, namely, that the everyday knowledge that the students bring may also transform and reorganise the curricularised knowledge of schooling.

Both insights are of particular relevance to the teaching and reception of canonised literary texts. Of specific interest to us are moments in the classrooms we observe when teachers create space for students to make connections between Shakespeare and their own everyday knowledge, and how educational drama helps foster such moments.

In probably the best-known area of Vygotsky's research, the Zone of Proximal Development (ZPD), he focuses on the ways in which learners make progress and how teachers might help them reach their full potential. In place of the traditionally retrospective approach based on testing what the child has already achieved, Vygotsky (1978, p. 86) proposes a form of supportive, collaborative pedagogy that anticipates what a child might achieve 'under adult guidance or in collaboration with more capable peers'. We argue in this Element that specific educational drama practices create the conditions whereby learning might be scaffolded[7] through collaborative, mutually supportive classroom activity.

Importantly in respect to our consideration of drama in relationship to English, Vygotsky's writings also begin to provide us with a theoretical paradigm for understanding the value of drama and role-play in education. From his observations of young children, Vygotsky proposes that play represents 'a leading factor in development'

---

[7] The more common educational term, first applied by Western Vygotskyan scholars Wood, Bruner and Ross (1976).

(Vygotsky, 1933) by which children develop the capacity to imagine situations outside of their immediate material context and experiences. For example, the moment a child at play is able to pretend a stick is a horse, 'one of the basic psychological structures determining the child's relationship to reality is radically altered' (p. 13). Vygotsky further draws attention to the roles children assume within their games; for example, if spontaneously pretending to be a mother, the child must play according to the socially and culturally defined rules that guide behaviour in their specific context.[8] In creating a reworking of what has been observed in real life, such play goes beyond the merely imitative, thus expanding the child's horizons by making intellectual, behavioural and emotional demands on the learner – a specialised form of ZPD:

> In play a child always behaves beyond his [*sic*] average age,
> above his daily behaviour; in play it is as though he were
> a head taller than himself. (1933, p. 17)

Of particular relevance to the teaching of drama in secondary schools, Vygotsky sees a link between children's play and the later internalised development of imagination (or 'fantasy') in adolescents, what he terms 'play without action' (1978, p. 93). He asserts that after puberty the imagination becomes a subjective form of thinking borne out of inner desires and the 'drive for creative expression' (Vygotsky, 1931). It enables 'higher syntheses of personality and world view' (p. 23), at once an intellectual and an affective psychological development. Although the links between these intimate adolescent fantasies and classroom drama are perhaps less clearly developed than other aspects of Vygotsky's writing, he is explicit in his promotion of acting, playwriting and dramatisation as potentially transformative learning experiences involving a complex interaction between language, semiotic tools and artefacts:

[8] In younger children rules often emerge as the play proceeds, whereas older children are more likely to agree on these in advance of the game commencing (Holzman, 2010).

> Drama, more than any other form of creation, is closely and
> directly linked to play, which is the root of all creativity in
> children. Thus, drama is the most syncretic mode of creation,
> that is, it contains elements of the most diverse forms of
> creativity. (Vygotsky, 2004, p. 71)

Myra Barrs (1987) develops Vygotsky's ideas about play and learning in
ways that are useful to contemporary English/drama practitioners. She
points out that drama and role-play combine 'action' and 'symbolisation',
making them a 'pivotal symbolic category and learning mode, drawing on
both the individual's powers of social action and on the normal capacity for
playing and imagining' (p. 215). She concludes that educational drama in
many ways mimics the learning processes that Vygotsky highlights in
young children's play. However, as Lois Holzman (2010) points out,
playing and learning are often regarded as antithetical in Western culture,
particularly for older children – an issue raised by teachers in our research.
Consequently, Joe Winston (2015) feels it necessary to defend the kinds of
'structured forms of theatrical play' (p. 77) deployed by the Royal
Shakespeare Company (RSC) in their workshops for teachers, by explicitly
rejecting the 'false but pervasive dichotomy between play and work' (p. 77).
Bound up with Vygotskyan understandings of play is a recognition of the
pleasurable nature of playful encounters with literature, encounters which
are effective in motivating the type of '"good learning"' that is 'always in
advance of development' (Vygotsky, 1978, p. 89). In Section 4 we present
examples from classroom practice which demonstrate the connection
between play, drama and learning and highlight the ways in which creative,
imaginative activity incentivises interpretative engagement with the plays
of Shakespeare.

Drama in English

Following on from Barrs, we propose a reader-centred approach to the
study of literary texts facilitated by drama. Such a pedagogy is underpinned
by an inherently sociocultural understanding of learning. It also draws upon
a long-standing relationship between English and drama both in practice

and policy. Official endorsement of drama as a pedagogic method within English can be traced back to the seminal Newbolt Report (*The Teaching of English in England*, 1921), which proposes play-acting as a method of teaching about dramatic literature, and includes references to both play-making and speech training. Nevertheless the association between English as a secondary curriculum subject and drama has not evolved in a straightforward manner, particularly in Britain. Although drama has been formally enshrined within each version of the NC for English (since 1989), it is always confined to the Speaking and Listening (S&L) programme of study. In the latest iteration of the NC (DfE, 2014) drama's role is limited to generating discussions about effective language use, and in the current version of the English GCSE examination S&L assessment is afforded little status and value. While retaining its uneasy position within English, drama has meanwhile separately developed as a popular subject discipline in its own right. Drama departments have been established in most British secondary schools, a situation that might not have been the case 'if English hadn't given time for it [drama] in the first place' (Neelands, 2010, p. 70). Nevertheless, as Jonothan Neelands points out, drama has rightfully remained integral to English studies specifically in terms of its 'content relationship' (p. 70) with literature.

Our intention in this Element is to reassert the broader conceptual connections between English and drama, particularly the role of drama in reading literature. To do so we draw on Barrs' (1987, p. 208) model by which she argues that reading requires enactment, whether that is as drama in the head or drama in action. She suggests that the text 'lives through us' (p. 208) whenever we tune 'our own voice to its demands' (p. 209). By the same token learners live through the texts they go on to create and this is why she characterises writing as '"drama on paper"' (p. 211). Barrs proposes that this 'ability to learn through enactment' is 'a fundamental mode of learning' (p. 215), but in its connections with play and imagination it retains an everyday quality. It is a way of learning that allows readers 'to use powers that they naturally possess' (p. 217), and as such she foregrounds their agency in the process.

Barrs views all aspects of English as 'involving the creation of fictional worlds and the assumption of roles' (Coles and Bryer, 2018, p. 56), thereby positioning drama as central to the reading and writing processes of the English classroom. Her model acknowledges the influential practices of Dorothy Heathcote, the internationally renowned drama educator. Heathcote is the leading proponent of 'drama as process' or learning *through* drama, one of two distinct traditions that have emerged during the development of drama as a discrete subject, the second being 'drama as product' or learning *about* drama. The shorthand term 'process drama' was coined by Cecily O'Neill (see Bolton, 1998, p. 189) to encompass and build on Heathcote's methods.[9] Heathcote's use of an imaginative, improvisatory approach to meaning-making is quite distinct from a view of drama as a performance art form that should be taught in the historical and cultural context of (a mainly Euro-American) theatrical tradition. The latter is skills-based with a fine focus on dramatic conventions derived from theatre practices, whereas in process drama 'the audience is the people who are creating it' and 'the makers of the meaning are the recipients of the meaning' (Bowell, 2006, pp. 27–8). The two traditions are often polarised in accounts of drama in education, perhaps more emphatically so in the UK than in other anglophone countries such as Australia and Canada (Fleming, 2019).

Because of its emphasis on learning *about* drama, it might be assumed that a drama-as-theatre-arts pedagogy offers the most appropriate approach when studying a Shakespeare play (or other dramatic work). However, as we exemplify in Section 4, process drama interventions offer powerfully productive ways for learners to engage with texts and co-construct literary knowledge. Process drama is characterised by the teacher's careful structuring of dramatic sequences, built across a number of lessons, utilising opportunities for participatory enactment, improvisation and interpretative approaches. Montgomerie and Ferguson's (1999) account of teaching reading through drama in a primary school setting offers a particularly clear example of what this might look like, although in the secondary English classroom such drama sequences are likely to be more closely shaped by the contours of the literary text.

---

[9] The complexities of Heathcote's methods and their evolution during her long and distinguished career have been discussed and theorised in detail elsewhere (see www.mantlenetwork.com).

In Vygotskyan terms, the 'process' in process drama affords learners opportunities 'to participate in a genuinely dialogic process' (Daniels and Downes, 2015, p. 106). It reflects the importance placed on collaborative and cumulative meaning-making through drama, what Harold Rosen (2017) refers to as 'moving towards collective wisdom' (p. 328), as opposed to focusing on the 'highly ordered and controlled' (p. 306) imperatives of theatrical production. We are not suggesting that the drama-as-theatre-arts model has no place in the study of dramatic literature, but rather that problems arise when theatre-based conventions are applied as a set of decontextualised exercises or one-off activities simply to add pedagogical variety.[10] Mike Fleming (2019) argues that it is possible to embed theatrical conventions such as tableau within process drama activity (and we provide an example of a teacher doing exactly this in Section 4). Tableau, also known as 'freeze frame' or 'still image', can be employed to freeze a moment in time 'to slow the action down, to step out of "real" time to explore experiences in more depth' (Fleming, 2019, p. 4). This is important in relation to literary study because to become immersed in a role does not imply that the learners' criticality is subsumed by their empathetic identification with the characters they inhabit. Heathcote (1991) suggests that learners in the drama mode are 'spectators of ourselves in ways often denied in a life situation, because we can distort time to give opportunity for reflection to be encountered' (p. 138); the action can be frozen, discussed, evaluated, replayed, replayed from a different character's perspective and so on. Working in this way enables learners to spectate critically and reflexively (Johnson and O'Neill, 1991).

In Section 4 we share examples of classrooms where English teachers have normalised the inclusion of process drama within English by fully integrating role-play with discussion, reading and writing activities. Drawing on Raymond Williams, we argue that role-playing and drama are part of 'the rhythms of everyday life' in a 'dramatised society' (1983,

---

[10] We have in mind publications which appear to present drama strategies in an alphabetical list of pick-and-mix conventions (e.g., Neelands and Goode, 2000) or as a way of enlivening atomised speaking and listening skills (e.g., DfES, 2003). For a more detailed critique see Pitfield (2006, 2020).

p. 12). While Williams' analysis focuses on the televised drama of his day, we believe the concept of a 'dramatised society' is even more applicable today, particularly in relation to the role-based cultural activities young people practise on digital platforms (Bryer, 2020). Drama has 'direct cultural continuity' (Williams, 1983, p. 14) with our own lives, in very much the same way that drama in the English classroom promotes cultural continuity with the real-world experiences of the learners.

Reader Response, Drama and Enactment

Our social constructivist understanding of the processes involved in knowledge acquisition and the teaching of curriculum content has direct relevance for the way in which we approach the reading of literature in secondary English classrooms. Barrs' focus on enactment in reading is in tune with those approaches to reading a Shakespeare play which, despite its canonical status, treat it as 'a script, a score for performance' (Stredder, 2009, p. 15), or as 'permeable, subject to interpretation and susceptible to current historical and cultural conditions' (Franks et al., 2014, p. 176). Such descriptions strongly suggest a two-way interaction or 'transaction', to use the terminology of the literary theorist Louise Rosenblatt (1994), one that 'involves both the author's text and what the reader brings to it' (p. 14). It is significant that Rosenblatt's notion of the reading transaction is similarly envisaged as a 're-enactment of the text' (p. 13); she describes the way in which the reader 'infuses his [*sic*] own voice, his own body, his own gestures – in short his own interpretation – into the words of the text' (p. 13). This is 'what each of us as readers of the text must do, even if . . . we remain entirely silent and motionless' (p. 13). She points out that the reader is also 'like a director' because they supply 'the tempo, the gestures, the actions . . . of the whole cast' (p. 13), and this taps into what cognitive psychologist Jerome Bruner (1986, p. 4) describes as the reader's psychological capacity to identify with characters and relate them to characters we 'carry unconsciously within us'.

There are unmistakable similarities between Rosenblatt's and Barrs' ideas of reading as enactment or drama in the head. However, Barrs goes further, citing the importance of utilising physicalised educational drama practices when learners read, and what she describes shares features with our concept of reading through drama. Learners physically assume the facial expressions and body language of their roles; they can explore a broader range of linguistic resources and 'stored (unconscious) knowledge' (Barrs, 1987, p. 215) which may otherwise remain untapped. Moreover, they are provided with the opportunity to play 'people with different perspectives on the world' (p. 216). As we have already indicated, Barrs sums up the crucial nature of enactment in Vygotskyan terms, as combining 'action' with 'symbolisation' (p. 215).

Building on Heathcote, Barrs (1987, p. 208) notes the 'ordinariness' of role-taking because it is what children do 'with ease' (1987, p. 207) in their play, and, like Vygotsky, she emphasises its cognitive potential in the more formal situation of the classroom. She is careful to draw a distinction between the actor's preparation for a role and what the learner does when role-playing. This echoes Heathcote's (1980) suggestion that learners are not subsumed by character; they simply wear the mantle of the role for a period of time, and by wearing a variety of mantles at different points during the reading of the play, they can, in Rosenblatt's terms, keep 'the whole cast' in view.

In this context, reception theorist Wolfgang Iser's (1989) description of the literary text as a playground in which the author and reader share a game of the imagination is a highly suggestive one. The reward of this textual game for readers is the richness of the meaning-making experience (Evans, 1987). This playfulness is possible because readers know that 'the textual world is to be viewed not as reality but as if it *were* reality' (Iser, 1989, p. 251), the 'as if' mode being a very familiar feature of drama (see O'Neill, 2015b). Even more fittingly, Iser suggests that textual gaps can be construed as 'play-spaces' (1989, p. 253). Our analysis in Section 4 illuminates how dramatic engagement with the plays of Shakespeare can enable learners to operate very directly within these play-spaces. In a distinct echo of reader response theory, Shakespeare academic Emma Smith fosters 'a reading of literature which . . . takes more seriously reception than the point of origin' (BBC Radio 4, 2019). She emphasises the reading potentialities afforded by the plays' textual gaps and indeterminacies. It is precisely the ambiguity, uncertainty and instability of Shakespearean drama which prompt imaginative engagement and 'provide space for us to think, interrogate and experience different potential outcomes' (Smith, 2019, p. 322). She describes this as a process for 'readers, playgoers and theatre-makers' (p. 322). To this list we would add learners in the classroom.

Yandell's (2016, p. 108) concept of 'embodied readings' produced within the social space of the classroom appears to overlap in an number of ways with our notion of reading through drama. In his social model of reading an important part of Yandell's school-based research focuses on a class of learners who are reading *Richard III*. In paying close attention to classroom interactions and the agency of learners in making meaning, he takes issue with reception theorists such as Iser (1978) who conceive of the reader as a lone entity. In doing so, Yandell makes the significant point that reading is instantiated as 'a collaborative or collective act' (p. 40) in most of the classrooms he observes, a perspective rarely reflected in official policy documents. Writing thirty years earlier, Emrys Evans (1987) also recognises the importance of classroom communality in the processes of reading and interpretation, drawing attention to the significance of reader-to-reader interrelationships, not just those between the author and the reader. Evans argues that classroom practices are socially situated, meaning that the interchange of learners' views opens up a range of relevant literary and lived experiences in relation to the text (p. 40). Yandell considerably expands such ideas in his simultaneously 'reader-oriented' (Giovanelli and Mason, 2018, p. 2) and socially oriented model of reading. Yandell also draws upon Bakhtinian (1981) concepts to evoke the heteroglossic, multivocal nature of learners' encounters with literature. Later, in Section 4, we too demonstrate how Mikhail Bakhtin's description of the novel as 'a diversity of individual voices artistically organised' (p. 262) can be (somewhat freely) adapted and applied to the drama-in-English classroom. Thus, in the study of Shakespeare, playwright, characters, teacher, learners and learners-as-characters share space and dialogue and it is this multivocality that is a key feature of reading Shakespeare through drama.

Some critics argue that drama-based approaches can divert attention away from the study of Shakespeare's text (see, e.g., Haddon, 2009; McLuskie, 2009). This is to misunderstand the way in which the drama of English lessons differs from the drama in the drama studio where a literary text may merely serve as a stimulus or jumping-off point. By contrast, 'reading through drama' pedagogy ensures learners' responses remain circumscribed and shaped by the fictional world the text creates (O'Neill and Rogers, 1994). Indeed, David Hornbrook (1988), the drama education-alist who has been perhaps the most outspoken critic of Heathcotean forms of process drama for their lack of attention to the scripts and conventions of theatre, advocates using drama when studying Shakespeare's plays, not to indulge in 'bardolatry' (p. 156), but to challenge it. He makes a strong case for 'more contextualised approaches to the plays' as well as allowing teachers the freedom 'to explore with their classes notions of Shakespeare as cultural product' as a way of reappropriating his 'powerful iconography' (p. 157).

In his critique of what he rather broadly refers to as 'New Iconoclast' literary critical approaches to Shakespeare, Jonathan Bate (1997, p. 335) implies that postmodern, pluralist readings of Shakespeare place too much authority in the hands of the reader: 'a leap from ambiguity to radical indeterminacy'. We want to make clear that the type of reading experience we have in mind is one 'shaped by the reader under the guidance of the text' (Rosenblatt, 1994, p. 12). Rosenblatt is explicit that these readings can be at the same time both diverse *and* 'responsibly self-aware and disciplined' (p. 129). We argue that reading through drama is key to this process. It is a collective endeavour which not only positions learners alongside the author, but also serves to authorise learners' own shared knowledge and interpretations (Jones, 2003). The text is not diminished by this sharing of space and authority with the learners; rather it ceases to be an abstract object of study and becomes incorporated into the cultural life of the classroom. In this way the reading of literary texts is less an act of cultural transmission and more one of cultural (and textual) production. Williams' (1977) description of the dual nature of literary texts is helpful in highlighting the inadequacy of a transmission approach to reading. He argues that, as works of art, literary texts are 'in one sense explicit and finished forms', but they are also waiting to be completed, to be made 'present, in specifically active "readings"' (p. 129). This is particularly pertinent to the types of engagement with texts that reading through drama facilitates, as the making and remaking of art 'is never itself in the past tense. It is always a formative process, within a specific present' (Williams, 1977, p. 129). As we attempt to illustrate in Section 4, drama encourages learners to interpret the text in different ways, or as Neelands expresses it, to tell their own stories in relation to the stories of others (O'Connor, 2010). It is our contention that the shared and contested interpretations arrived at through drama in English serve to deepen engagement with the script rather than divert attention away from it.

'Active Shakespeare' Pedagogies and Definitions

Accounts of English teaching typically identify the early 1990s as a pivotal moment in Shakespeare pedagogy, one characterised by the development of performance-based approaches both in the UK and in the USA (see, e.g., Kress et al., 2005; LoMonico, 2009; Olive, 2015). Emerging alongside radical shifts in academic Shakespeare criticism, the 'active Shakespeare' movement is most commonly associated with Rex Gibson, whose Cambridge Shakespeare and Schools Project James Stredder described in 2009 as 'the most influential specific initiative in Britain in the last twenty years' (Stredder, 2009, p. 5).[11] Gibson's Leverhulme-funded project offered teacher secondments, extended and 'one-off' professional development events; produced a journal (Gibson, 1986–94) and a project report (Gibson, 1990); inspired the publication of several Gibson-authored monographs (e.g., 1997, 1998); and culminated in the influential Cambridge Schools Shakespeare editions of the plays (now in their third edition), a number of which were edited by teachers who had themselves been project participants. Further cementing Gibson's British legacy was the glowing endorsement for his project's 'exciting' methods of teaching Shakespeare by the government-appointed body tasked with the production of England and Wales' first NC for English (DES/Welsh Office, 1989, paragraph 7.16). Over the ensuing years, however, the term 'active Shakespeare' has come to signify an ill-defined spectrum of physicalised, performance-based approaches – often simply counterposed to so-called

---

[11] Again, a transatlantic phenomenon, of which new historicism and cultural materialism are two key examples. See Dollimore and Sinfield (1985).

desk-bound teaching methods (e.g., as is strongly implied in the RSC's 'Stand up for Shakespeare' slogan adopted in 2008).[12]

Here we want to compare four different, internationally recognised versions of 'active Shakespeare': Gibson's original project, the method associated with the Folger Shakespeare Library in Washington, DC, the Playing Shakespeare initiative developed by the Globe Theatre in London and the RSC's 'rehearsal room' approach promoted through their UK-wide schools outreach programme, the Learning and Performance Network (LPN). We particularly focus on the ways in which they conceptualise the relationship between drama and reading. Additionally, since each of these organisations involve – or have involved – working with teachers and schools, we are interested in considering the different models of professional development offered. This is of particular relevance to the data we present in Section 3, where outcomes from teacher interviews suggest a disconnect between the services offered by creative organisations and teachers' practical needs.

All four initiatives take as their starting point the fact that Shakespeare wrote plays to be performed. The late Rex Gibson was famous for beginning his teacher workshops with a collective 'oath' chorused by participants holding copies of plays aloft: 'This is not a text; this is a script.' His American contemporary, Peggy O'Brien, the director of education at the Folger Shakespeare Library, likewise emphasises the performance aspects of Shakespeare's writing in her introduction to the Folger Shakespeare Set Free series:

> The man wrote *plays*. So is this about *acting*? No, it's about *doing*. Students get his language in their mouths, take on the work of actors and directors, get to know a play from the inside out. (O'Brien, 1993, p. xii)

Not surprisingly, the professional theatre companies foster a similar performance-related perspective on Shakespeare. According to Globe education advisor Fiona Banks (2014, p. 3):

---

[12] See Winston (2015), pp. 13–16.

> Reading his plays without any form of active engagement,
> without his words in our mouths and emotions and actions
> in our bodies, is like trying to engage in a piece of music by
> looking at the notes on the page but not listening to the
> music itself.

Or, as the RSC's 2008 manifesto puts it: 'The best classroom experience we can offer is one which allows young people to approach a Shakespeare play as actors do' (cited in Winston, 2015, p. 13). Although Brian Cox's NC working group hailed active Shakespeare as an innovative alternative to 'once-traditional … desk-bound' teaching methods (DES/Welsh Office, 1989, paragraph 7.16), it is worth pointing out that this type of approach was not new, even in 1989. Pedagogical attentiveness to the performance aspects of Shakespeare plays, both in Britain and in the USA, can be traced back at least to the beginning of the twentieth century. Joseph Haughey's (2012) overview of archived issues of US publication *English Journal* between 1912 and 1917 reveals experimentation with performance-oriented approaches to Shakespeare study by a number of contributors. These early twentieth-century articles represent a surprising range of drama pedagogies extending beyond basic 'acting out' of scenes to embrace role-play and improvisation. Meanwhile in Britain, the English Association, founded in 1906 with the purpose of promoting English as a subject in schools, sought to afford Shakespeare the recognition due as the national poet by publishing a pamphlet (1908) recommending an embryonic version of 'active methods' alongside an emphasis on the desirability of seeing a live theatre performance. Newbolt's (1921) report into the teaching of English in the socio-political aftermath of World War One not only established Shakespeare at the heart of school English, but also promoted the idea that its linguistic challenges ('so remote as to be an unfamiliar tongue', p. 312) might be largely overcome by treating the plays primarily as drama scripts. The report references the 'interesting experiments' (p. 103) of Henry Caldwell Cook at the Perse School in Cambridge, ideas which clearly helped shape Newbolt's recommendations regarding the teaching of Shakespearean drama. John A. Lester's (1926) contemporary account of Cook's 'active approach to Shakespeare' (p. 448), published by the American National

Council of Teachers of English, suggests that Cook's influence extended beyond England.

Since Newbolt the twentieth-century history of Shakespeare teaching has been marked by sporadic publications promoting a 'performance-based' approach, two good examples being *Inspirational Teaching* (1928) emerging out of George Mackaness' 'Play Day Movement' developed in Australia; and A. K. Hudson's (1954) *Shakespeare and the Classroom* published in the UK. Miriam Gilbert, who ran Shakespeare workshops and seminars for high school teachers at the University of Iowa from the early 1980s, asks why performance-based approaches seem destined to be 're-discovered' from one era to the next (Gilbert, 1984, p. 601). It is a question that interests us too, and it is one we come back to later.

Although the starting points of the four more recent projects are similar, there are subtle but significant differences in their pedagogies. The majority of the sample activities Gibson offers in his seminal text, *Teaching Shakespeare* (1998), are recognisably rooted in educational drama (e.g., role-play, tableau, improvisation), but they also include a range of artistic and imaginative modes (e.g., creative writing, film, drawing, collage) by way of exploring plot, characters, language and themes. Gibson himself makes clear that his conception of 'active' extends beyond the merely physical: 'Active methods comprise a wide range of expressive, creative and physical activities' (1998, p. xii). Gibson further characterises 'active' as demanding a high level of intellectual challenge, imaginative participation and emotional engagement on the part of learners. In a clear echo of constructivist understandings of learning, Gibson's key 'principles' include making Shakespeare 'learner-centred' (p. 9) and 'social' (p. 12). Furthermore, Gibson's belief that scripts need to be 'completed by enactment of some kind' (p. xii) on the part of the reader or performer is suggestive of reader response theory.

The Folger approach partly arose out of O'Brien's organisation of Shakespeare performance festivals for schools, underpinned by her belief that 'the playwright had something to say to each one of these kids, and they each brought something to him' (O'Brien, 2009, p. 29). Possibly as a consequence, O'Brien's definition of the Folger approach places greater emphasis on physical activity and movement than that of Gibson:

> Don't worry about that stodgy academic notion that the body and intellect can't be engaged simultaneously, that students moving about a classroom can't possibly be *really* learning anything. Make no mistake: learning Shakespeare through *doing* Shakespeare involves the very best kind of close reading, the most exacting sort of literary analysis.
>
> (O'Brien, 1993, p. xii)

Like Gibson, O'Brien rejects any notion that physical activity and intellectual endeavour sit in opposition to each other, but the precise relationship between drama and reading as a process is left vague. In the thirty years since the publication of *Shakespeare Set Free*, a distinctive 'Folger Method' has evolved, summarised by O'Brien (2019) as a basic set of eight 'foundational principles' and nine 'essential practices'. The primary underlying principle is that Shakespeare's language 'is not a barrier but a portal'; teachers are urged to reject 'tidy explanations', to 'amplify the voice of every single student' and to position themselves as 'architect' of learning rather than 'explainer'. Whilst the principles echo those in *Teaching Shakespeare*, the published list of practices (e.g., 'tossing words and lines', 'two-line scenes', '20 minute plays', 'choral reading') is progressively organised and more systematised than anything Gibson proposed. The reading-drama nexus that is our prime focus of interest is implied in the one-page 'Philosophy of Teaching and Learning' published on the Folger website,[13] but not explicated:

> The Folger continues to produce – with and for teachers – ever-evolving sets of language tools, active close reading strategies, performance techniques, and pathways through the plays that are energizing and fun, and that *relentlessly* focus on text.

[13] www.folger.edu.

The possibilities opened up by 'active close reading strategies' here are nevertheless somewhat constrained by the same declaration's overall focus on 'text', its subsequent promise of unspecified 'rigour', and its later reference to 'citing textual evidence' which sits oddly in a statement of philosophy. What 'kids' bring to Shakespeare, to borrow O'Brien's earlier phrase, is not immediately apparent from this.

Whereas it is evident that both O'Brien and Gibson bring their former teaching experience to bear on their Shakespeare approaches, the RSC and the Globe's educational programmes are rooted in theatre practice. In recent years the two education departments have marketed their own distinctive brands of active Shakespeare in the form of the 'rehearsal room techniques' developed by the RSC and the live, creative Shakespeare experience offered by the Globe Theatre in London, explained in detail on their respective websites and in recently published texts by project practitioners (Banks, 2014; Winston, 2015).[14] At the heart of the Globe's educational programme is the physical space of the replica Elizabethan theatre itself and the opportunity for school students to watch a live professional production, 'the perfect way to introduce young people to Shakespeare ... to break down walls to cultural access and empower teenagers to develop their creative curiosity' to quote the website. Indeed, key components of the online learning resources offered by the Globe revolve around streamed productions, including interviews with directors and other key theatre personnel, actors' and creative designers' blogs, and a 360-degree virtual tour of the theatre building. Banks chooses to open her monograph celebrating the work of the Globe education department with the words: 'The Globe is a space of experiment and discovery' (2014, p. xi), thereby locating 'creative Shakespeare' (the term she employs to describe their brand of 'active Shakespeare' and the title of her book) firmly in the Globe's unique theatrical environment. 'Creative exploration' she states categorically, is to be 'found in the rehearsal room' (p. xi). Nevertheless, Banks, like Gibson before her, does not restrict her definition of 'creative Shakespeare' to physical activities: 'creative approaches are active, physically and/or intellectually', whether experienced in an 'empty space' or 'at

[14] www.rsc.org.uk/education; www.shakespearesglobe.com/learn.

a desk' (p. 5). Throughout the collection of predominantly drama-based teaching ideas and activities that make up the bulk of the publication, Banks advocates a playful, exploratory approach to the plays, stressing that the text itself is not 'sacred in any way' (p. 7). Although in her introduction Banks gestures towards sociocultural understandings of learning ('no student is a blank canvas', p. 2), she later firmly positions 'the text [as] central to learning' (p. 6) and emphasises the 'universal' (p. 10) nature of Shakespeare's stories and characters. These apparent contradictions make it difficult to determine the way in which Banks is conceptualising the relationship between reader and text in her account of the Globe's approaches to teaching Shakespeare. Indeed, Banks herself compares her publication to a 'cookery book' (p. xi), inviting the reader to select individual activities and adapt in the way one would a recipe. It thus conveys the impression of being driven by a practical 'what works' approach as opposed to a theoretically coherent pedagogy.

In contrast, what is notable about the RSC's education work is the focus on developing a consistent pedagogy rather than a set of methods, very possibly as a result of their ten-year academic collaboration with the University of Warwick (from 2005). With the explicit aim of theorising the RSC's signature 'rehearsal room' approach, Jonothan Neelands and Jacqui O'Hanlon, of Warwick University and the RSC respectively, argue that it 'takes the artistry and critical engagement of its pedagogy beyond the conventional uses of "active methods"' (2011, p. 240). They draw direct links with 'social constructivist' (p. 244) understandings of learning and emphasise 'participation, collaboration, trust and mutual respect' as key elements (p. 246). In their independent evaluation of the LPN at the end of its first three-year cycle Thomson et al. (2010) emphasise the collaborative, even 'democratic' (p. 14) nature of rehearsal room pedagogy: 'Learners act as co-constructors of the meanings created through work on a Shakespeare text. Ensembles are built in and through the time/space of the rehearsal room' (p. 16). It is, according to Winston (an academic partner from the University of Warwick), a pedagogy which has 'emerged organically and fluidly, through practice and over time' (2015, p. 37). In mapping out the evolutionary journey of the RSC's approach, Winston identifies Cicely Berry, former RSC voice coach, as the 'seminal' influence (p. 43). Her work with professional actors focused on physicalising Shakespeare's language – a method celebrated for successfully breaking down oppositions between the intellectual and the physical. While there is some evidence of cross-fertilisation between Gibson's project and that emerging out of the RSC education department in the mid-eighties,[15] Winston draws a clear distinction between Berry's and Gibson's ways of approaching Shakespeare and consequently their respective influence on the RSC's signature pedagogy. While acknowledging Gibson's work in schools as 'ground-breaking' (p. 37), Winston contrasts Gibson's 'conscious, rational world of teacher planning' and 'restraint' (p. 44) with Berry's 'playful edginess and deep theatricality' (p. 44), suggesting in his historical account that Gibson's 'active Shakespeare' legacy has left much less imprint on the educational work of the RSC than Berry. Sarah Olive (2015) is critical of what she sees as an act of 'appropriation' (p. 114) on the part of the RSC, a broader rebranding exercise she has provocatively summed up in the following way: 'To paraphrase the British department store Marks and Spencer's now-infamous marketing of their chocolate pudding, "it's not *just* Shakespeare, it's *RSC* Shakespeare"' (p. 119). Certainly the RSC makes a bold claim for the educational value of its own-brand 'rehearsal room' techniques on its website: 'Research suggests that young people get the most out of Shakespeare's plays when they experience rehearsal room approaches,' almost suggesting an RSC monopoly on success. The 'remarkable' benefits ascribed to this way of working include a mixture of Shakespeare-specific gains ('Improved experiences of, and opinions about, Shakespeare') and broader educational advantages (e.g., 'Helps young people to express themselves and their ideas more clearly'; 'Improves student confidence').[16] Nevertheless, a crucial recommendation arising out of

[15] For example, the first issue of Gibson's Shakespeare and Schools 'Newsletter' (autumn 1986, p. 6) bears a prominent photo of Berry, announcing that she was to lead a workshop for the Shakespeare and Schools team of seconded teachers in the following spring (1987).

[16] Evidence from predominantly quantitative research by academics from Warwick University (Lindsay et al., 2018) and the RSC's own end-of-project attitudinal surveys (2016).

Thomson et al.'s (2010) independent review points to the need for LPN practitioners to pay greater attention to working with students at an interpretative level, noting a tendency 'to avoid grappling with the big ideas of the plays and the ways in which they might connect with students' own lives and experiences' (p. 22). As we have already indicated, this denotes a significant area of interest for us. What students already know and what sets of cultural experiences they bring to Shakespeare are issues rarely referenced in Winston's (2015) comprehensive account of the RSC's work and only hinted at in Neelands and O'Hanlon's (2011) article.

Offering professional development for teachers forms a significant feature of all four projects' missions. The Globe Theatre practitioner team responsible for providing student workshops and training for teachers comprises 'actors and directors ... clowns and writers' (Banks, 2014, p. 2) whose job, the Globe website promises, 'is to unlock Shakespeare's language, themes, characters and stories in an active and creative way'. Fundamentally, the Globe's educational vision is one of cultural access and enrichment (Yandell et al., 2020), enabling large numbers of young people to see a live performance of Shakespeare as part of its 'Playing Shakespeare' outreach programme.[17] The Globe offers one-off teacher professional development sessions and school-based workshops for groups of students in preparation for this visit to the theatre. The RSC's LPN programme developed between 2006 and 2017 was structured in a markedly different way to that of the Globe's 'Playing Shakespeare' initiative. Supported by funding from both public and private institutions and working in collaboration with the University of Warwick, the LPN rested on establishing long-term relationships with participating schools and teachers with the overall aim to make lasting pedagogic interventions in the way

---

[17] The scale of the Globe's programme is impressive. Central is the annual spring season 'Playing Shakespeare with Deutsche Bank' production, a different play each year shortened and adapted specifically for secondary school audiences. In the first ten years (since 2007) the Globe allocated around 140,000 free tickets to state-funded schools in London and Birmingham (Yandell et al., 2020).

Shakespeare is taught.[18] According to Thomson et al. (2010, p. 5), it offered teachers and students 'significant intellectual and practical resources' over a three-year period. Where the two programmes overlap is in their claim to 'unlock' Shakespeare by using the 'rehearsal room' skills and expertise of theatre practitioners. We find this proposition somewhat problematic as it potentially underestimates the specific professional contributions English and drama teachers are capable of making in the production of new forms of Shakespeare pedagogy. Banks (2014) suggests that there is no such hierarchy of knowledge in the relationships between the theatre practitioners and teachers, as 'every session relies on the interaction between teacher, students and play. It is no accident that "teacher" is first on this list' (p. 1). Nevertheless, the centrality of the teacher as professional and expert is most clearly articulated in Gibson's work:

> Teaching is a professional activity in which each teacher makes considered judgements to decide what is appropriate for each particular class of students. Professionals do not seek a universal recipe . . . the professional teacher's skill lies in the subtle and thoughtful adaptation of content and method to suit the actual circumstances.
>
> (Gibson, 1998, p. xi)

Gibson's Shakespeare and Schools Project relied on the enthusiasm of a national network of teacher participants, a result of offering full-time secondments to practising teachers to work with English and drama colleagues in their own locality over the period of a school term. Publications, such as the project journal (1986) and the end of project report (1990), although edited by Gibson, consisted almost entirely of contributions by classroom teachers sharing ideas and experiences.

---

[18] Two main sources of funding for the LPN came from the Paul Hamlyn Foundation and the Arts Council England. Reduction in arts sponsorship following the 2008 global financial crash has necessitated a reconfiguration of the RSC's education work (Winston, 2015).

In the following sections we raise concerns around different models of teacher development and explore associated questions about professional confidence in relation to pedagogical experimentation. Given widespread acceptance that performance-based approaches offer rich and engaging ways of teaching Shakespeare,[19] we ask why some English teachers are so hesitant in employing drama methods. Why, to reiterate Gilbert's (1984) question, do active Shakespeare methods need to be rediscovered by successive generations of educators? With reference to examples of classroom practice and by paying attention to teachers' own reflections, we propose 'reading through drama' as a more sustainable form of active pedagogy.

3 Shakespeare in Practice: Institutional Constraints and Teacher Agency

One of Kate McLuskie's criticisms of active Shakespeare as characterised in published accounts is its proponents' relentless focus on the positive. 'No-one', she says, 'ever describes a bad class' (McLuskie, 2009, p. 131). While McLuskie is writing largely from a higher education perspective, it is a complaint Esther Schupak (2018) echoes in her discussion of performance-based professional assumptions and practical constraints drawn partly from her own experiences of teaching Shakespeare in US and Israeli high schools. We recognise the grain of truth in these objections, and in this section we aim to offer a more nuanced account of teachers' and students' experiences with drama-based approaches, one that acknowledges the quotidian realities of teachers' lives at an institutional and a broader political level. Drawing on transcripts of videoed lessons and interview data, we offer a sample of curricular Shakespeare interactions for analysis, all of which take place in the context of England's highly regulated, outcomes-focused education system (albeit prior to further curriculum and assessment reforms in 2014). We are, inter alia, interested in the ways in which teachers and

---

[19] An assumption which underlies English teaching manuals published in the UK. See, for instance, Davison and Daly (2019) and Fleming and Stevens (2015).

learners negotiate competing discourses around school Shakespeare and to what extent they can make sense of it as both a curricular and cultural entity.

Heritage Shakespeare: Discourses of Deficit

Underpinning much of the debate about the curricular value of Shakespeare runs a discourse of deficit, particularly in relation to learners' cultural lives outside school. In effect this rests on assumptions that the majority of young people lead culturally impoverished lives and that a canon-rich curriculum will serve to compensate for this. In Britain Shakespeare has been invoked by politicians as the saviour of the poor and dispossessed, able to liberate them from the 'shadow of ignorance and the chains of dependency' (Gove, 2010). This cultural deficit view, however, is not limited to the speeches of politicians and can be detected in the published views of liberal commentators and even arts practitioners. One such commentator is Michael Boyd, celebrated for developing the education department of the RSC in his role as artistic director between 2002 and 2012 (see Winston, 2015). In his contribution to a collection of papers written in anticipation of NC revision ('The Heart of English', 2012),[20] he asks, 'How do children and young people get introduced to Shakespeare or theatre or the arts? Who unlocks the complex canon of literature and culture on offer to everyone; who helps them develop an appreciation of the arts and culture?' He recommends a version of 'cultural inheritance' to which all should be entitled: 'all of our children should also be given access to the kinds of literary, cultural and artistic opportunities that independent schools will see as an automatic right for their students'. Boyd's proposition amounts to what Sinfield (2004, p. 215) terms 'left culturism', a belief that education can bring about upward mobility by means of an individual's cultural transformation. As an ideological position this is fraught with problems, not least in the way it devalues (and, in its extreme forms, negates) any cultural activity practised by young people themselves, especially that which deviates from the dominant forms. In Boyd's cultural universe teachers and arts practitioners are positioned as

---

[20] https://heartofenglishblog.wordpress.com

keyholders to canonical riches, in effect limiting young people's engagement in school to 'appreciation' of other people's culture.[21]

Unsurprisingly, pragmatic questions about enabling all children to gain access to this authorised version of cultural knowledge have preoccupied British teachers since the inception of the NC. It has contributed to what Gunther Kress et al. (2005) regard as a 're-agenting' (p. 14) of schools, where professional attention has shifted away from curriculum design and analysis (the 'why?') onto the practical development of specific pedagogical methods (the 'how?'). 'Active Shakespeare' was thus recommended by the authors of the first NC (DES/Welsh Office, 1989) as a seemingly straightforward practical solution to complex cultural problems exacerbated by summary imposition and compulsory assessment. One of our ongoing concerns is whether active Shakespeare pedagogies sufficiently acknowledge 'Shakespeare' as a complex cultural sign, one that represents a site of struggle, even alienation, for many young people. Malcolm Evans (1989, p. 34) uses the term 'incrustation' to capture the sense in which Shakespeare becomes weighed down by socio-historical layers of signification, like shells sticking to a rock. In what follows we attempt to probe active Shakespeare's capacity to chip away at these cultural accretions.

It has for many years been a commonplace amongst English teachers in Britain that the mere mention of Shakespeare by a teacher will, as often as not, be met by a chorus of adolescent negativity, prime complaints being that it is for 'posh' people, has no relevance and will be boring (see, e.g., Galloway and Strand, 2010; Neelands, 2008; Yandell, 1997). It is a phenomenon with which teachers in our research are all too familiar. Here, for instance is Beth, the head of English at Eastgate School:

Beth: . . . there is to an extent a cultural thing that, you know, obviously the sort of fetishism of Shakespeare and that can actually have quite a powerful effect and that can put some students off . . . I think you do have a big thing about Shakespeare. It's difficult

---

[21] Boyd does propose in the same statement that children should be culturally productive, but he frames their reception of canonical works purely in terms of passive appreciation.

and I think a lot of students will say that without even knowing anything very much about Shakespeare. I mean I started doing *The Tempest* with my Year 9s a couple of weeks ago, we did something as an introductory activity ... it didn't explicitly say we are doing *The Tempest*. But the kids said, 'Oh, well, are we doing Shakespeare? Are we doing *The Tempest*?' as if to say Shakespeare is boring, you know, and that was before they read a word ...

Given how common this type of response is on the part of learners, it is surprising how rare it is for 'active Shakespeare' publications to make explicit reference to Shakespeare's monumentalism. Both Gibson (1998) and O'Brien (2019) refer to it obliquely when talking about the importance of demystifying Shakespeare ('Give up Shakespeare worship' is one of the Folger principles), but with little direct evaluation of drama-based methods' effectiveness in achieving these aims. One of the few active Shakespeare proponents to address it more explicitly as a real issue to be overcome is Stredder (2009) in *The North Face of Shakespeare*. He acknowledges that the prospect of studying Shakespeare is for many students akin to contemplating the perilous ascent of a remote, icy rock face. For Stredder, the solution lies in 'open[ing] up the texts as fields of play' (p. 6), a physically and intellectually active process which should enable students to claim ownership of the plays and overcome feelings of intimidation. Neelands and O'Hanlon (2011) also raise it as an issue, briefly wondering where learners' negative views come from. In response, they too promote active Shakespeare – more precisely, the RSC's ensemble/rehearsal room approach – but their stated purpose, 'reclaim[ing] Shakespeare as the birthright of the disadvantaged and oppressed' (p. 245), appears closer to Boyd's ideological position than Stredder's. Surveys of students involved in the RSC's LPN programme (Galloway and Strand, 2010; revised in 2011, see Winston, 2015) do indeed record some attitudinal improvement following engagement with the project. Nevertheless, when evaluating the first three years (in 2010), the researchers concluded that it is ultimately hard to shift young people's deep-seated antipathy to Shakespeare even in the context of a well-resourced, long-term performance-related project such as that the RSC offers.[22]

Insights we have gained from our research over many years lead us to remain unconvinced that drama-based methods in themselves – or attendance at a live performance as per the Globe programme – can provide a universal antidote to the very specific cultural baggage accruing to Shakespeare. We have interviewed many students for whom classroom Shakespeare has not been a liberating or 'democratising' experience, even in cases where their teachers have employed some form of active methods (see, e.g., Coles, 2013). As Sheila Galloway and Steve Strand (2010) imply, unpicking these entrenched attitudes is more complicated than some commentators allow (and, we would add, made more resistant to change by the constraints of the assessment system). By way of illustration, we want to consider a moment of classroom interaction during a Year 10 lesson at Parkside School, followed by a short exchange taken from a small group interview at Eastgate School.

An overview of our sample of lesson observations indicates that it is rare for questions of Shakespeare's iconic status to be raised explicitly as part of the official discourse, a phenomenon that remains consistent even across our wider data set. One such moment, however, arises in Pip's Year 10 *Romeo and Juliet* class during the final lesson while she is setting up the formally assessed coursework essay (an analysis of Act 1, scene 5). Before examining this classroom exchange, we want to emphasise that Pip's classroom is one in which study of the printed play text has been supplemented with lively drama activities and the viewing of Luhrmann's film.[23] Indeed, preparation for the summative assessment has involved students acting and directing their own versions of the key scene across the two previous lessons. However, Pip takes the opportunity to draw attention to Shakespeare's

---

[22] Researchers undertook to update the 2010 survey results a year later and reported statistically significant improvements in student attitudes to Shakespeare – for details, see the chapter co-written with Strand in Winston, 2015, pp.133–58.

[23] Baz Luhrmann (dir. 1996). *William Shakespeare's Romeo + Juliet.* Twentieth Century Fox.

cultural status in a way which is, despite the initial invitation to open it up for discussion, ultimately non-negotiable:

Teacher:	. . . in your conclusion . . . you need to sum up your ideas OK, so address the title, again, so, 'How are the themes of love and hate dramatised in the scene?' Sum up the points you've made, talk about Tybalt, talk about Romeo, discuss how the theme presented, themes presented here, are still relevant today and what you might say about Shakespeare's works. So, thinking about why Shakespeare is still studied in school. Why 400 year old, why is he important for us, what we've been looking at today? [a couple of students begin to murmur in dissent. Teacher raises her voice] And even if you don't like him –
Muna:	[interrupts] Why is he?
Student:	[unidentified] Yeah!
Teacher:	Why is he? Let's have a discussion about it?
Abeola:	No!
Teacher:	Well, everyone apart from Abeola wants to have a discussion about it apparently!
Ben:	He's famous!
Teacher:	I don't think that's anything to do with it. Why, why particularly, perhaps not just Shakespeare, why has this story stayed so popular over the years? What is it about it?
Student:	People growing up?
Abeola:	Because this happens a lot in real life!
Teacher:	Right, explain.
Abeola:	Oh my god [smiles].
Muna:	[incredulous tone] What, killing yourself because Juliet loves another man, right?
Teacher:	Maybe that exact story doesn't happen in real life, but I think I know what Abeola's getting at.
Ezekiel:	It's a good story.
Teacher:	OK, it's a good story, right. Why is it a good story? Why do so many millions of people 400 years ago and today read or go and see the play or the film and really enjoy it? Why, even if

	you didn't particularly enjoy it? Why do we enjoy it? What, what is it about it that's enjoyable? OK? [indicates student with hand up]
Student:	Coz Shakespeare is famous.
Teacher:	So is that why we enjoy the story, though, because Shakespeare is famous? Right, think between the lines –
Anjna:	It's a catchy story.
Joe:	It's got lots of things like love and fighting and death.
Teacher:	Right, it's got everything, it's got the ingredients of a really great story, hasn't it? We've got love, we've got hate, we've got fighting, we've got violence, er, think about when we first started when you were thinking of the openings of films that are really dramatic and are action-packed … So, it's about characters, it's about themes, it's about emotions that are expressed in the play that people today can relate to as much now as they could do back then. Everyone's been in love, everyone's been hurt, everyone's had an argument with somebody they're close to and so you can relate to these kinds of things. OK, that's my argument anyway, and I think that it's a valid argument, so something that you might think about putting in your essay, OK. Right. We're through with that now. Are there any questions about the essay?

It is notable here that students do challenge Pip's view of Shakespeare's cultural importance – a rare moment of dissent in her classroom. But for all Pip's attempts in previous lessons to frame *Romeo and Juliet* in terms her students can connect with (e.g., drawing heavily on the 'pop' cultural references of the Luhrmann film), she is by the end of the unit of work unprepared to concede any cultural ground.[24] There seems to be an underlying assumption on her part that students ought to have emerged from the particular pedagogic experience uniformly appreciative of the play's

---

[24] A position perhaps exacerbated by her concern about GCSE assessment – even though the official examination board rubric at the time did not preclude students expressing their personal opinion about Shakespeare.

relevance to their lives. So, although she does at one point in this sequence suggest that it is a legitimate response not to enjoy Shakespeare ('if you didn't particularly enjoy it'), this is immediately contradicted by her question 'why do we enjoy it?', the apparent universality of a positive response signalled by her use of the first person plural pronoun. Furthermore, she refuses to acknowledge that Shakespeare's celebrity might have any significance in perpetuating his apparent popularity. She avoids holding up to any scrutiny Shakespeare as a cultural construction and how that reputation has been shaped and disseminated. The emphatic discourse markers used by Pip at the end of the sequence ('OK'; 'Right') are further strengthened by her statement 'we're through with that now', forcefully communicating the end of any further discussion. Yet Muna's challenge to universalist critical discourses indicates that for her this is far from a satisfactory conclusion to several years' worth of compulsory contact with Shakespeare.

An equally interesting moment arises during a small group interview with four students held at the end of Beth's sequence of active, participatory lessons on *Henry V* with her Year 10 class. For Joshua, Shakespeare's monumental reputation is still very much intact: 'He's famous, he's a big man, he's like an antique, a legend sort of thing.' In fact, Joshua's comments spark an interesting debate when he spontaneously goes on to link Shakespeare and the Bible, the latter being, in his opinion, even more deserving of a place in the curriculum ('it's the same language but the Bible's more interesting than Shakespeare'), a point immediately queried by his classmate Owsun. Joshua attempts to push the argument further:

Joshua:	But you don't need Shakespeare, do you? It's not going to help us in the future.
Owsun:	But it's a good thing to learn, it's a good thing to learn!
Jane Coles (JC):	Why is it a good thing to learn?
Owsun:	Because of the language and the heritage.
Chaz:	It's not my heritage!
Karen:	You're British, aren't you?
JC:	Why, that's a really interesting comment, why did you say that? You said, 'It's not my heritage.'

Chaz: It's not my heritage. I'm not related to Shakespeare . . . I'm not
            really bothered, coz this country, really, it gets on my nerves,
            man, and soon as I reach eighteen, I'm leaving. But I still say,
            why Shakespeare? [unclear] Why is he the one?

Contestations over 'heritage Shakespeare', however ill defined here as
a concept, come to the surface of the students' conversation in a way we
have not witnessed during lessons, even in the context of Beth's consciously
learner-centred classroom. This snatch of dialogue offers a glimpse into the
way Shakespeare appears to be linked to differing notions of Britishness in
all four students' minds, reflecting perhaps the shifting complexities of often
hybridised identity in modern urban Britain, here crossing boundaries of
faith, ethnicity and social class. The tone of the argument, initiated by
Joshua's heartfelt promotion of the Bible, quickly becomes quite heated,
culminating in Chaz's angry renunciation of Shakespeare along with 'this
country' (rather frustratingly, the interview was terminated at this point by
the signal for change of lesson). That students are rarely provided with
formal curriculum space to unpick the way canonical texts relate to their
personal histories and beliefs means that the curriculum is likely to remain
disconnected from students' lives, the point of it never made clear.

Teacher Agency and Accountability: 'How Much Time Can We Spend on the Fun Stuff?'

Understandably, educational projects linked to high-profile arts institutions
such as the Folger, the Globe and the RSC are less concerned with
addressing notions of Shakespeare's iconic status than with setting out
pedagogical agendas which seek to engage with issues around access,
entitlement and demystification of theatre as a cultural practice. The RSC,
for example, sets great store by drawing a distinction between the rehearsal
room and a 'conventional classroom' with desks (Winston, 2015, p. 43). In
the light of this emphasis, it appears to us that the RSC's relentless focus on
the value of theatre-inflected, performance-oriented models of pedagogy is
in danger of creating a discourse of deficit in relation to English teachers'
existing pedagogical knowledge and experience, a discourse which

acknowledges neither the situation 'on the ground' in schools nor the range of interconnected factors that bear down upon decisions about practice. Schupak (2018) identifies a number of key challenges for English teachers in their attempts to adapt for seminar and classroom settings the 'performance pedagogy' (p. 163) associated with the Folger, the RSC and the Globe. In doing so she rather surprisingly highlights English teachers' lack of acting skills as an issue, recommending practical theatre courses as professional development. As such, we believe this represents a misunderstanding of the nature of drama-based Shakespeare pedagogies, which are, after all, directed towards *learning* rather than theatrical performance. As we outlined in Section 2, this approach draws on the everyday quality of drama and has affinity with the role-taking of play. Of necessity, the teachers in our study work on a daily basis in classrooms with desks, operating within the constraints of curriculum and lesson planning; they are also working with students who do not come, as actors do, with an advance knowledge of and interest in the script. So, Jamie, a newly qualified teacher (NQT)[25] at Downham Fields School, cautiously speculates whether 'finding ways you can integrate it [drama] as a bit of a lesson' might help him to overcome the challenges. Another Downham Fields English teacher, Paul, who has five years' teaching experience, adopts a different approach. Making a conscious effort to introduce drama into his repertoire of literature teaching methods, he books the drama studio for a series of drama-based English lessons with a Year 9 class (fourteen-year-olds). Rather than emphasising the everydayness of drama, the new arrangement signals to the class its specialness.

Of relevance when considering Paul's approach are the questions raised by Anton Franks et al. (2014) concerning the effects on teachers' professional subjectivities of the move from classroom to rehearsal room spaces and how the rehearsal room setting might facilitate changes to teachers' pedagogic practices and shifts in their 'sense of what is possible in the classroom' (p. 172). Paul's experiences demonstrate the ways in which such shifts are shaped by and must still fit within the existing contextual

[25] At the time this was the official designation for a teacher in the first year of teaching. Newly Qualified Teachers are now known as Early Career Teachers (ECTs) and retain this status for two years.

boundaries dictated by national policy and local priorities. The suggestion of Franks et al. (2014) that the effects of 'rehearsal room pedagogy might go beyond the learning of Shakespeare and reach into the teaching of poetry and prose fiction' (p. 180) chimes with Paul's efforts to utilise drama methodology in the space of the drama studio also when reading a novel with his students. Certainly, the move from classroom to drama studio seems to hold more significance than a simple matter of addressing the lack of physical space in his English classroom, and he reflects on the distinction between the two learning areas: 'The change was with the drama room – that is seen as being a very imaginative space. I do like the whole ritual, the rite of passage of moving down there.' This brings to mind Fleming's (2019) idea of ritual as an important feature common to both children's play and drama activity, particularly as Paul's later reflection on his own drama in English practices focuses on his need to control less and provide his students with more opportunities to play. As far as the learners' experience of English is concerned, Paul is positive about the potential of the drama studio to provide an 'imaginative space'; 'I do like' suggests that, for him too, this space for drama (both physical and imaginative) might offer a welcome degree of pedagogical freedom, a position which echoes the responses of the teachers in the research of Franks et al. (2014). In one of the lessons Paul reinforces this idea when he urges the students to inhabit the 'imaginative space' of the drama studio. Unfortunately, this also hints at the corollary, the English classroom as an unimaginative space.

Paul acknowledges that he finds it a challenge to manage the students' freedom of movement and their playfulness in the larger space of the drama studio in contrast to the more regulated and controlled atmosphere that he fosters in his regular classroom. We sense that, by separating the space for drama activity from the space for the other aspects of English, he is finding a way to prevent the former from influencing the latter. For example, one drama-based lesson begins in the English classroom, but this is to allow him to give a PowerPoint presentation of 'Top tips for effective improvisation'. Even though the rest of the lesson happens in the drama studio, a place his students associate with their discrete drama lessons, Paul does not reach across the disciplinary boundaries to elicit their prior drama knowledge of improvisation protocols. Throughout the period of his experimentation with drama methods, behaviour management remains an ongoing concern and he cancels two drama-based lessons at short notice, deciding that the move to the drama studio has proved too disruptive, and noting in an email to Maggie, 'as I am now straying from the SoW [scheme of work] and Learning Objectives I am conscious of the "drama learning" losing meaning'. Despite the number of drama-based activities he has tried out, Paul records only one in his written SoW, saying he prefers to leave it to the other members of the department (who will teach the scheme at a later point) to decide whether and how they will employ drama. This indicates his view of drama activity as additional to rather than an embedded part of his English planning and teaching.

Paul's experience with his Year 9 class happens at a point when English teachers had been freed from the tight constraints of KS3 SATs, but his anxiety about alternative ways of assessing reading is clear. He has taken on responsibility for introducing a new government initiative, Assessing Pupils' Progress (APP), at both the school and the local authority levels.[26] Paul initially justifies his adherence to the APP model by stating that the English department's teaching of reading at KS3 is not 'systematic' enough. Interestingly, though, after teaching a small number of drama-based lessons he begins to question this:

Paul: Actually, I kind of had a bit of a realisation the other day which was, yeah but this [APP] is just an artificial assessment tool anyway, you don't necessarily need to come back to that assessment tool. What they're doing [the Year 9 class in drama], and I do really believe this, what they're doing is much more in keeping with, if you like, a real engagement with the text. That's much more 'real reader'.

[26] The New Labour government imposed the APP in order to fill a perceived post-SATS assessment void. It employed a highly atomised set of criteria or 'Assessment Focuses' (AFs) collated into separate grids for Reading, Writing and Speaking & Listening, which encouraged a box-ticking approach. Nevertheless, English teachers were required to expend considerable time and energy grappling with APP, only for it to be rejected in its entirety by the Conservative-led coalition government that succeeded New Labour in 2010.

He sets 'real' reading and 'organic reading' in opposition to the skills approach of APP: 'Do the AFs develop reading skills? Yes. Is that how children read? Probably not.' Yet, later, when giving his reasons for exclusively focusing his SoW on the development of APP-compatible reading competencies, he draws attention to the officially 'visible' nature of this document, referencing its wider audience and thus highlighting the significance of the accountability mechanisms by which English teachers are bound. One such high-stakes mechanism is the system of governmental school inspection (Ofsted), and Downham Fields is expecting notification of Ofsted's arrival at any time. Despite the positive points he identifies in some of the drama-based lessons, once he is faced with preparing the class for their forthcoming internal assessment task, Paul takes the decision to halt any further drama activity.

Professional confidence is clearly an important factor in shaping attitudes towards reading through drama practices, as a discussion between Jamie and his colleague Chloe, another early-career English teacher at Downham Fields, further demonstrates. The 'bigger picture' at the time – the relatively recent abandonment of KS3 SATs and the introduction of a revised NC for English (QCA, 2007) which proclaimed creativity as one of its underpinning concepts – had promised a freeing up of the curriculum and a greater degree of autonomy for English teachers. However, the assessment and time pressures of GCSE remain uppermost in the minds of these teachers when interviewed:

Chloe: Yeah, first of all Year 10, it feels like there's a lot to get through and at the end of that you have to have a piece of coursework. So, when I taught *Romeo and Juliet* last year for the first time I did a drama lesson, I did two drama lessons. I went on a really good course with the RSC for a day, um, and I really enjoyed it but I couldn't see actually what they'd [the learners] got out of it that they directly needed. I could see generally what they got out of it, but this time round I didn't even end up doing those lessons because I was worried about time and how that ... even though I could see why ...

Jamie: . . .the pressure's been really on us, hasn't it, with the Year 10s, I feel, and the coursework . . .

Chloe: Year 10 it feels quite difficult in terms of what they've got to get done, and also, you know, when you're an NQT you feel those pressures more because you want them to deliver. So Year 9, I do think there is more time, um, but yeah behaviour isn't very good.

It is important to note that, in a previous career, Chloe was an actor in a theatre-in-education company that toured schools performing Shakespeare plays and running workshops. She is an enthusiastic and popular young English teacher whose lessons are lively and inclusive, and in addition she has benefitted from RSC input. She is predisposed to this way of working, yet it would seem that her experiences of utilising drama in the study of a Shakespeare play have been overwhelmed by acutely felt pressures, as a novice teacher, to ensure that learners 'deliver' their achievements, her use of this word suggesting how the commodification of learning has been imbibed. What is 'directly needed' for examination assessment therefore appears to be the only valid indicator of learners' understanding of the play and of the teacher's effectiveness in teaching it. Chloe's comments reveal an emergent view of classroom drama as diversionary in the context of a results-driven agenda.

English teachers' hesitation to devote time to drama activities does not go unnoticed by students. In a small group interview at Woodside Boys' School, Joel (a Year 11 student about to take his GCSE examinations) shows he is well aware of the curriculum and assessment messages that are directly and indirectly communicated by teachers:

Joel: That's really important because like with written work, if we're not enthusiastic about written work, they're not going to take away the written work and give us something else to do, but with a drama activity, if we're acting up that day, they're just gonna take that away so they see it as like a –

Ricky: – privilege.

Joel: Yes, exactly, they see it as a privilege, but in reality it's exactly
           the same as written work. If anything, they're not holding it high
           enough in terms of esteem because drama activities help you just
           as much as written activities; I just don't think they understand
           that.

Although across our entire data set we have evidence of teachers who
point to the positive effects of active methods on student engagement and
learning, Joel's comment nevertheless rings true. It suggests that, if
teachers perceive drama as peripheral rather than integral to practice in
English, on the few occasions when it is deployed, behaviour management can become a very real issue. This in turn reinforces concerns about
its use and relevance. In addition, as Joel highlights, when drama
connotes a reward for accomplishing those elements of the subject
invested with greater importance, it becomes something that is easily
removed in response to learners' behavioural misdemeanours. In contrast, Chloe and a fellow English teacher, Emmanuel, at Downham
Fields perceive negative attitudes as emanating from the students rather
than their teachers. Chloe and Emmanuel have become highly sensitised
to the voices of learners in their GCSE classes who challenge the teacher
for spending time on drama activity rather than on conventional forms of
assessment preparation. Emmanuel attributes such attitudes to students'
'preconception of the subject and obviously what's expected of them',
yet neither he nor Chloe question how these preconceptions might have
been produced.

   Whilst Joel rejects a notion of drama as peripheral to English and
recognises the part it has played in his learning, there is also a suggestion
that he understands the constraints English teachers face. This is apparent when he expresses his concerns that 'in English leading up to that
Year 10, Year 11 stage where you have to know what an examiner wants
you to do', there is a conflict between the narrow requirements of GCSE
English literature assessment, identified by Joel as the expected
response, and the more wide-ranging interpretative activity of drama
in the English classroom. This concern is echoed by Beth, the head of
English at Eastgate. Like Chloe she has attended a day's INSET run by

the RSC which has prompted her to develop a very successful drama-based activity working with a scene from *Henry V*. However, when Beth is preparing her students for the formal GCSE assessment task, her essay support sheets are immensely detailed and dense, including a pre-prepared essay plan, photocopied scenes taken from the Cambridge Schools edition and quotations already marked by the teacher alongside handwritten marginal notes. Such heavily mediated, overly scaffolded assessment preparation sits in abrupt contrast to the open-ended, drama-based work that formed a central feature of her previous lessons. It, perhaps unwittingly, signals to students that the entire endeavour might be too difficult for them (for a more detailed analysis, see Coles, 2013). This is not because Beth underestimates her students; rather, as she makes clear in an interview, her real dissatisfaction is with an assessment system which assesses understanding of a play script solely through a written response, reducing a Shakespeare play to an 'exam text'. These are very real tensions which Neelands and O'Hanlon (2011), in their account of the LPN, similarly acknowledge. They suggest rehearsal room pedagogy also struggles to bridge the gap between providing young people with access to a Shakespeare play and finding ways of developing the skills 'and the socio-historical knowledge' necessary to grapple with it in a more analytical, assessment-friendly way (p. 244).

Chloe's experience demonstrates that the specific institutional context is also a key factor in what happens in classrooms. The English department at Downham Fields is a youthful one and is experiencing overt intervention from the school's senior managers, resulting in a forced move from a long-established tradition of inclusive 'mixed ability' classes in English to a form of setting (or tracking) in anticipation of an Ofsted inspection.[27] It is this sort of managerialist interference at whole-school level that Ken Jones (2003) suggests has repercussions for both the relationship English teachers have with their subject and learners'

---

[27] As recently as ten years prior to the research period, 'mixed ability' (or, more accurately, mixed attainment) was the usual method of organisation for English classes in state schools, particularly so in London, until it came under systematic attack from successive governments.

experiences of English in lessons. Despite Chloe's strong background in drama, the educational narrative that examination results alone measure the worth of both teachers and learners holds sway, and that such success can only be achieved by 'teaching to the test'. Chloe's concerns are indicative of how far assessment has come to dominate the curriculum, a situation that has only intensified in the intervening decade and is as applicable to primary as it is to secondary schooling (see Barrs, 2019). The normalisation of 'teaching to the test', accompanied by officially endorsed systems and rubrics for doing so, leads to an impoverishment of curriculum and serves as a barrier to experimentation. It is also an important factor in the de-professionalising of English teachers, compromising their role as pedagogic decision makers: with regards to the study of literature, it invests them with the authority to impart only particular textual interpretations that will serve examination purposes.

Professional Development and Institutional Support

Shona, an Advanced Skills Teacher (AST)[28] at Woodside Boys' School, is an advocate for active and drama-based approaches in English lessons, yet she is well aware of the challenges for English teachers in retaining their sense of professionalism:

Shona: We lose confidence then in the value of this work [drama in English], even though instinctively we know it has great value for our students, we lose confidence in our ability to explain its value in a culture which is ... which can often feel, you know, this sort of notion that you've got to be able to show progress for everybody by the end of the lesson. We lose confidence in our ability to explain how that is visible in this kind of lesson [a drama-based English lesson].

---

[28] The role of the AST was introduced in 1998 to reward excellent teachers in state schools in England and Wales who, rather than following management routes to promotion, chose to stay working in classrooms whilst tasked with sharing good practice with teachers in their own and other schools.

The 'notion' she refers to is derived from the Ofsted framework for school inspections by which inspectors make high-stakes judgements about the extent of learners' progress even though they do not have to observe whole lessons or sequences of lessons. Her repetition of 'we lose confidence' highlights the negative effects of heavy regulation and the persistent targets and outcomes culture.

In contrast to Chloe and her colleagues, Shona's practice, however, is supported by a very stable, experienced English department which has successfully warded off senior management and local authority demands to relinquish a long-held commitment to mixed-ability teaching. It has also been invigorated by the school's 'Learning Community' initiative comprising six staff groupings which emerged out of the Creative Partnerships programme (for which Shona was a school co-ordinator), rather than being imposed institutionally.[29] The development work of the groups has continued even after the external funding has dried up, and the teachers have published a book about their experiments in utilising creative teaching and learning approaches in a range of subject areas. Nevertheless, in an interview one comment in particular reflects how Shona too is forced to grapple with the pressures arising from institutional systems of accountability: 'How much time can we spend on the fun stuff and how full should the book be of long pieces of writing?' As a core subject there is no denying that English carries a heavy responsibility, its GCSE results being 'double-weighted' in the league table rating of secondary schools in England. Here Shona is pointing to the problems of the ephemeral nature of drama and the drive to offer to external audiences something to show, in the form of written work, for the learners' activity in the drama in English lesson. Thus, discourses of professional accountability demand that 'commitment and experience within practice' are 'sacrificed and compromised for impression and performance' (Ball, 2004, p. 9). So, Claire, another of the early career English teachers at Downham Fields, hints at the prevalence of such a discourse

---

[29] Creative Partnerships, a well-funded flagship project of the New Labour government, designed to bring creative professionals into schools to work with teachers. From 2002 to 2011, more than 2,700 schools across England were involved in the project.

when she states: 'English essentially has always been about reading and writing, that's what you get your GCSEs for; you don't get it for drama.' This stance is in stark contrast to Barrs' (1987) account of drama and role-taking as integral to both reading and writing – and, in reality, does not do justice to Claire's very creative classroom practices.

Shona's unusually dismissive characterisation of drama as 'the fun stuff' is surprising as elsewhere in the interview she offers a very different account of the role of drama in studying Shakespeare:

Shona: It's what they [the learners] bring back to the next lesson from having done all of that [drama work] is sometimes most powerful. You know, lovely things like why would Anne agree to marry Richard [in Shakespeare's *Richard III*]. It's so much easier to write about that if you've been Anne and he's bullied you into it than to try and write that from scratch just because Miss says, 'Anne agrees; Anne is bullied.' Well, why does she? That can come later, I suppose. It doesn't necessarily have ... you don't necessarily always have to have got to that point by the end of that fifty-five minutes [the length of a lesson at Woodside].

Here Shona highlights the 'long game' nature of literature learning and the potential of drama to capture and sustain students' interest. In this respect her focus on character echoes Gilbert (2009): 'for many students, questions begin with characters ... That is, what grabs students – and what bothers them – is what the characters are like and why they are behaving as they do' (p. 92). Nevertheless, it is the aforementioned throwaway comment that demonstrates how the relationship between classroom practices and imposed constraints impinges on the consciousness of even an experienced and confident proponent of reading Shakespeare through drama. Whilst we fully acknowledge that it is no simple matter to 'read off' from research data the extent to which external pressures impact on pedagogical beliefs and classroom practices (Jewitt and Jones, 2008), these examples suggest wider discourses inevitably permeate the English classroom, sometimes in very significant ways, and therefore cannot be discounted.

These constraints inhibit English teachers in their use of active approaches and raise pertinent questions about how they and their students can be best supported to develop reading Shakespeare through drama practices. The RSC, for example, has focused its education resources on 'working in sustained relationships with teachers' (Neelands and O'Hanlon, 2011, p. 245), to develop the 'range of sophisticated teaching strategies' (p. 241) and skills that Neelands and O'Hanlon claim are necessary for the successful employment of rehearsal room techniques (see also p. 244). Over a three-year period training was offered to selected teachers from supportive schools in a wide network of hub and cluster schools.[30] An RSC education practitioner, Tracy Irish (2011), makes the point that embedding 'the risk-taking dialogism of active approaches to teaching a Shakespeare play' requires 'support and trust from senior leaders and policy makers' (p. 8), and this highlights the importance of investment in professional development at both the local and the national levels. The independent evaluation of the LPN (Thomson et al., 2010) advises a move to practitioner research (from action research) in the Postgraduate Certificate part of the training because it shifts attention from a preoccupation with the '"what works" discourse' (p. 32) on to why it works, and it promotes understanding of practice at a theoretical rather than an activity level. As a paradigm, practitioner research is collaborative, respectful of teachers' professionalism, expertise and agency, and, as highlight:

> places more emphasis on the teacher thinking through what it means to do 'insider research'; this not only opens up the question of taken for granted assumptions but also of what kind of evidence is required in order to find out what has happened as a result of the new strategies being tried. Thomson et al. (2010, p. 32)

There are parallels to be drawn with the type of professional development processes that evolve over time and that support 'the intellectual creativity of [English] teaching' (Daly, 2004, p. 196) by enabling teachers to critically interpret their experiences through 'instruments for reflection' (p. 196). For

---

[30] The selected 'lead teachers' could opt to study for a Postgraduate Certificate in the Teaching of Shakespeare, accredited by Warwick University.

teachers who are seeking to experiment with drama methodology, Heathcote's (2015) 'security thresholds' (p. 19) model is just such a reflexive instrument: it is 'bottom-up' (teacher-led) and designed to facilitate self-scrutiny (see Pitfield, 2020). Linzy Brady (2009), a researcher with the Shakespeare Reloaded project, persuasively argues that, for teachers already operating in a highly centralised curriculum and assessment system, 'top-down' teacher development initiatives which ignore the specific and the local are inappropriate.[31] In this respect her Australian-based research chimes with evidence from our case study schools. She makes a strong case for 'teacher learning that is anchored in collaboration, ongoing research and [crucially] authentic educational contexts' (p. 336). She also proposes that in such a model the English teachers' 'repertoire of pedagogical knowledge for effective teaching' (p. 343) is the galvanising force. This resonates with Irish's (2011) account of Karen, a teacher in a London comprehensive school who embraced the LPN training, disseminating it via in-service training (INSET) and enabling 'top-down' (RSC-led) and 'bottom-up' development approaches effectively to work together. Shona's experience in taking ownership of the Creative Partnerships initiative at Woodside Boys, and its application to the reading Shakespeare through drama practices of her own classroom, has a similar flavour. Nevertheless, Thomson et al. (2010) draw attention to issues associated with the cascade model of training the RSC employs, particularly highlighting the '"dilution" effect in the LPN as the work ripples out from the central RSC experience' (p. 26).

[31] The 'Shakespeare Reloaded/Better Strangers' initiative was originally conceived as a research collaboration between the University of Sydney and a local secondary school. Its stated purpose is to explore new approaches to teaching and learning Shakespeare, to 'combin[e] the experience and skills of academics and school teachers to produce educational activities for the classroom and professional development workshops' (see https://shakespearereloaded.edu .au). Now in its fifth phase of development, the project has developed an outward-facing website with the intention of forging a 'community of research and knowledge dissemination' (Colnan and Semler, 2009, p. 6).

With this in mind, in Section 4 we move on to provide examples of English teachers who have found ways to successfully integrate drama methods into their pedagogy, developing active Shakespeare practices that are sustainable and attentive to their specific school contexts.

4 Shakespeare in Practice: Reading through Drama

In the previous section we acknowledged the realities of teaching Shakespeare within highly regulated contexts. We now analyse instances where teachers – working in these same national contexts – have succeeded in opening up opportunities for learners to explore a Shakespeare play through collaborative, dialogic enactment. We examine ways in which these approaches foreground learners' own beliefs, experiences and lives outside school as a vital part of the meaning-making process.

Role-Play and the Dialectical Production of Character
Beth's approach to teaching a Shakespeare play mounts something of a challenge to conventional assumptions about 'active Shakespeare'. Throughout Beth's Year 10 scheme of work, *Henry V* is conceived as a performance text, yet all of the lessons we observed take place in a classroom crowded with desks, allowing for very few occasions when groups of students are physically on their feet.[32] Beth's pedagogy is also noteworthy in the way it effectively decentres the printed text. Until the point at which explicit preparation for the assessed coursework essay begins, Beth combines film, role-play, classroom enactments and periodic close attention to extracts from the printed play script. This approach raises interesting questions about what counts as a text and what we mean by 'reading' as a practice in literature classrooms.

Beth introduces her students to *Henry V* through the medium of film and to the figure of Henry using a still image captured from Kenneth Branagh's film version depicting the king's first entrance at the opening of

---

[32] In British schools a scheme of work spans approximately six to seven weeks of lessons.

Act 1, scene 2.[33] She asks students to analyse the photocopied screen grab in pairs, her instructions positioning the students as 'viewers of Henry', a perspective that encourages a degree of critical distance: their impressions of Henry avoid stock responses around conventional literary notions of 'character' (What is he thinking? What does he feel?) and instead focus on the trappings of kingship and on Henry's entrance as a dramatic moment:

Teacher:	. . . Other words people came up with? Richard?
Richard:	Powerful.
Teacher:	Brilliant! Why powerful?
Richard:	Because he made an impression; he's coming out of darkness, the doors opening, it's lightening him up.
Dexter:	He's wearing a robe.
Teacher:	He's wearing a what?
Dexter:	[gestures with his hands] He's wearing all robes, like a cape –
Student:	[interrupting, humorous tone] Cape! He's not Superman, you know!
Dexter:	[deliberately finishing what he was saying] They make him look scary.
	[Several students start to shout out]
Teacher:	[amused] Because robes are always scary? [she gestures to the next student]OK, guys! Ade, what else have you got, please?
Ade:	I just put powerful and scary.
Teacher:	Powerful and scary. OK. Bode, what did you put?
Bode:	I put dark, manly figure.
Teacher:	Brilliant, yep, OK. Cem?
Cem:	The light's on him; it means God's on his side.
Teacher:	Fantastic. I really like that: the light's on him so God's on his side. I like that one a lot. OK, Karen.
Karen:	Secrecy because he's in shadow.
Teacher:	Brilliant, secrecy, I like that.

---

[33] Kenneth Branagh (dir. 1989). *Henry V*. Universal Pictures.

The lively buzz in the room and the eagerness with which students contribute during this section of the lesson suggest that working with a visual image has released them from the rather more intimidating prospect of analysing printed text, particularly at this early stage of studying a play. Basic, descriptive comments ('he's wearing a robe') quickly shift to comments on a more interpretive level, such as the comments offered by Karen and Cem. Attention is drawn to the theatricality of the moment in the way the lighting falls on the actor, frozen here on the verge of moving out of darkness into light. Above all, Beth is happy to present the central character, Henry, as intriguingly enigmatic – there is no rush to simplify and neatly categorise as is the practice we have commonly observed in other classrooms (see Coles, 2009). This introductory activity marks Beth's first step towards constructing a reading of Henry which begins to capture some of the ambiguities inherent in Shakespeare's portrayal of the king. Broadly speaking, Beth's approach here is calculated to develop over time into a consideration of Henry as a complex, dramatic figure whose actions have significant political, social and personal consequences in the course of the play. Unsurprisingly, in later stages of the scheme of work Beth selects for close analysis the language of Henry's motivational speeches prior to the Battle of Agincourt (Act 4, scene 3) and his savage threats of violence before the walls of Harfleur (Act 3, scene 4).

Having analysed the image of Henry's entrance, the students go on to watch the opening scenes of Branagh's film, stopping at the entry of the Dauphin's ambassador. Beth recaps the various arguments proposed by characters in the first two scenes to justify declaring war against the French. As she does so, she takes the opportunity to make an explicit connection with Cem's earlier comment about God being on Henry's side. Already there is a sense that knowledge in this classroom is not the sole preserve of the teacher; students' contributions are respected and meanings made collaboratively.

In the next lesson we observed, Beth commences with a drama activity, picking up the play at the point of the French ambassador's entrance (2.1.233). As she explained in a later interview, the original idea for dramatising this moment came from a 'fantastic' professional development event run by the RSC that she had attended. What follows provides a good example of an experienced teacher able to select and adapt performance-based approaches to suit her own pedagogic purposes and institutional context. By locating the drama activity in the physical space at the front of her classroom, it requires little in the way of organisational disruption. Importantly, because it is not constructed as a 'special event' it enables Beth to integrate drama, writing and reading deftly into the natural flow of her English lesson.

Beth begins by asking for a volunteer to come forward as Henry and another to be the French ambassador presenting the king with a mystery gift:

Teacher:	Right, OK, Henry now comes in, OK, and I want someone here to stand at the front and be Henry. Yeah. OK, Owsun. [Owsun gets up and moves to front] And I want somebody else to come [turns to Owsun] come and stand over here where there's a bit of space. OK, Henry has just come in, walked in through this door. He's now um, he's now standing there and the French ambassador – I need a volunteer to be the French ambassador [a few students make unintelligible, stereotypical 'French' sounds]; don't worry about the language, you're just going to give Henry a present.
	[Several students put up hands and call out]
Unur:	I don't mind!
Teacher:	OK, Unur [he gets up and comes to the front. Teacher gives him a large parcel wrapped in brown paper] OK, the French ambassador ... How do you think the French ambassador is feeling as he walks up to Henry to give this present?
Unur:	Scared and nervous.
Teacher:	Scared and nervous. Right. Why are you feeling scared and nervous?
Unur:	Because he's afraid he might get killed.
Teacher:	And he's representing his country. Kadife, what were you saying?
Kadife:	Might get killed.
Teacher:	Might get killed. Good.
Richard:	He shouldn't; he's an ambassador.

Teacher:	Yup, he shouldn't do, because he's an ambassador; he should be protected, but he's a bit worried. OK. What do you think, Graham, what do you think is the message you, er, he is going to say? He's already had a message that Henry wants to invade France. What do you think the French ambassador is going to say to that?
	[Various students make stereotypical French sounds]
Teacher:	Listen! Dexter?
Dexter:	We don't want war; we want to make peace.
Teacher:	We don't want war; we want peace, OK. But what else might, probably, the king of France think if the king of England writes and says, I want your country?
Student:	[in French accent] Idiot!
Teacher:	Idiot. Perhaps.
Ade:	War!

Beth invites predictions as to the contents of the parcel (suggestions include 'a bomb', 'a head'), then Unur, in character as the ambassador, bows and passes over the box. Owsun is directed to open the present, which he does in suitably dramatic fashion, revealing tennis balls. Quelling the inevitable chorus of disappointment, Beth leads a whole-class discussion as to what tennis balls might symbolise; all students are then individually asked to write down what they think Henry's response is likely to be before sharing their answers with the class:

Teacher:	... We'll hear a few ideas, what's Henry going to say and then ... I'm then going to very, very quickly show you a little bit of what Henry does actually say ...
Ade:	[reading in role] 'He's suggesting I should go play tennis. This is a great insult. If he wants to play with me, we'll play on the battlefield.'
Teacher:	Brilliant. Yeah. [indicates another student with hand up] Right, OK, Dexter? OK, listen!
Dexter:	[reading in role] 'How dare you! The cheek! I should kill you for the thought against a king!'
Teacher:	Good. Right, Karen?

Karen: I don't want to.

Teacher: Go on! Or shall I read it then? [moves across to Karen and
            reads her work] 'Is this a joke? OK, if he wants to stick tennis
            balls, um, then off with his pig head. He's got another think
            coming! I want his head and when I do, I'll play tennis with it
            and let that be a warning to him!' OK, excellent!

Following this, students can compare their predicted responses in character
as Henry with Shakespeare's play script, first by watching how this scene is
portrayed on film before looking more closely at photocopies of Henry's
speech in print. Role-play, film and play script are inextricably linked here
in the reading process, overlain with a playfulness which invites a high level
of creative – and, we would argue, critical – engagement. The kind of
enactment observed in Beth's classroom is inherently Vygotskyan in that
students draw on a range of semiotic affordances (e.g., gesture, facial
expression, pose) as they grapple with what Yandell (2016, p. 69) calls the
'doubleness' of role-play. In imagining themselves as a fictionalised, historically remote figure, learners need to draw on their own everyday lives,
emotions and experiences to flesh out their performed role. It involves
a complex dialectical interplay not only between scientific and everyday
knowledge but also, as Yandell puts it, between difference and continuity.

    On occasion the outside world of an East London urban classroom inserts
itself more overtly into the realm of curricularised study. During a later stage
of the *Henry V* scheme of work students are in small groups discussing what
Henry might say to rally his troops on the eve of the Battle of Agincourt in
Act 4, scene 3. Kadife is prompted by her group's ongoing exchange of ideas
to ask Beth: 'Were people living in England in them days, were they all
Christians?' Overhearing, Cem pursues this line of thought and asks Beth
what would have happened in Henry's day to someone who was not
a Christian, which prompts some discussion about historical context. Later,
when performing his motivational speech to the class, Unur incorporates the
words 'Do it in the name of Allah.' No doubt the literary and historical
inaccuracy of Unur's invocation might concern some teachers of English.
Indeed, criticism of active Shakespeare often focuses on unresolved tensions
between certain types of reified knowledge and experience (see, e.g., Haddon,

2009; McLuskie, 2009). Rather, we believe that the kind of learning happening in Beth's classroom draws attention to Unur's agency as a learner; he has grasped the significance of faith in bolstering Henry's geopolitical ambitions and makes sense of that in his own terms. In doing so, he is behaving simultaneously as a social actor and a dramatic actor (Franks, 1996; Neelands, 2009). Students' own beliefs and cultural understandings are incorporated into the social fabric of Beth's classroom to the extent that identity and difference form an important dimension in the dialogic production of meanings.

We also want to draw attention to the production of 'character' in Beth's lessons as it forms a significant component of the students' study of the play. As noted earlier, Gilbert (2009, p. 92) points to the usefulness of employing character as a point of entry into Shakespeare's plays, even at undergraduate level: 'more immediate than questions of structure and more accessible than the language'. While eschewing Bradleyan-inflected notions of 'character study', Gilbert argues that the ostensibly dry politics of the history plays become less remote to students once they can recognise the personal dimensions. In Beth's classroom 'character' as a literary and dramatic entity is particularly complicated. Henry exists in multiple forms: as a film role (played by an actor who may or may not be recognisable to students); as a figure captured in a monochrome frozen image; as a living representation personified by Owsun; and subsequently as a role reimagined by every student in the class. Shakespeare's Henry in the form of a printed script puts in occasional appearances and somewhere at the back is Henry the historical figure, alluded to sporadically in students' questions about life and times 'in those days'. In this context, it is not surprising that Unur feels confident in introducing the class to Henry as a Muslim orator. Clearly, however, this is not the version of cultural heritage promoted by politicians.

Exploring Sexual Ambiguity through Dramatic Play

Beth's careful and responsive structuring of the learning sequence is apparent in her seamless integration of the different modes of English as she moves between discussion, drama, writing and reading. This is also a feature of Shona's pedagogy with her Year 7 class (twelve-year-olds) at Woodside Boys School, as is the dynamic interrelationship between everyday and curricularised knowledge that we have drawn attention to in Beth's lessons. Both position the development of literary knowledge as an ongoing process, recognising that learners' understandings of and relationship to the texts studied are constantly evolving.

We now want to focus in some detail on one of Shona's lessons. In particular, we want to highlight the way she connects the play script with students' own experiences and concerns by drawing on their propensity for 'zestful imaginative play' (Bruner, 1986, p. 4) as the wellspring of cultural production. Shona begins by allowing her students a degree of licence in imagining what is going to happen in *A Midsummer Night's Dream (MND)* when Titania awakes under the influence of a powerful love juice. Shona does not reveal what animal Titania falls in love with; instead, she pre-frames[34] a reading of the scene by utilising dramatic play, allowing the students to choose a beast for themselves (they mostly opt for monkey or ape). This approach enables her to bring learners' own experiences and concerns gradually into 'knowing engagement' (Neelands, 2009, p. 175) with the script; as we demonstrate in what follows, this also means that the sexual nature of Titania's relationship with the beast is not glossed over in favour of the fairy and magical elements, as is often the case when the play is taught to adolescent readers (see Smith, 2019). In contrast with Beth's way of working, Shona reorganises the classroom for this lesson by pushing the desks back. This space, marked out by a circle of chairs, facilitates students' experimentation with the scene through play and movement. Her students are accustomed to such arrangements: across a range of lessons we have observed her Year 7 class engaged in drama activity at their desks (Shona and the students refer to this as 'desk drama'), in groups utilising the spaces between the desks, and sometimes spilling over into the corridor.

In setting up the drama, Shona reads aloud Oberon's speech (2.1.179–82):

---

[34] Adapted from Jackson (2007), this term describes the way in which learners can be prepared in advance for their experience of a dramatic scene or theatrical event.

The next thing then she waking, looks upon –
Be it on lion, bear, or wolf, or bull,
On meddling monkey or on busy ape . . .
She shall pursue it with the soul of love.

She then prompts students to speculate what might happen when the plan is enacted. Assigning half the class to the role of Titania and the other half to the creatures Oberon lists, she frames the drama through a combination of narration and direction. For instance, she guides Titania's actions in this way:

Teacher: This room is going to be transformed into a woodland and it's going to be transformed by music. I'm going to play some music to suggest this room is a magic woodland. And as Titania you're going to need to search around the magical woodlands and find somewhere to fall asleep. You can fall asleep sitting up in a chair. Or fairies might even sleep standing up, who knows how they sleep, they may lie down? That's going to be up to you. You're going to find a place to sleep and while you're asleep you're going to imagine that the flower juice goes on your eyes so that when you wake up the first thing that you see you're going to fall in love with.

Imagining and transformation are therefore central to the lesson and take on an embodied quality through, for example, Shona's speculation about how fairies sleep. Nevertheless, when Shona allocates the roles in this all-boys' class, there is some resistance from a number of the learners who are assigned the Titania character in the face of mockery from others who are to play the animals. The requirement to play a female character is plainly an issue for some, and Shona probes this later as part of their reflection on the scene.

Initially Shona allows the students to play quite freely with their characters as they move around the circle, with the proviso that they should 'get inside their own head, doing their own drama to begin'. Santos, for instance, appears absorbed in his role as Titania as he moves outside of the circle, but not outside of the drama, and sits on a table, swivelling round, to face one way then the other, in time to the music and in a leisurely yet regal fashion, until he finds a comfortable position in which to lie down. His actions are carried out without reference to or engagement with others in a classroom now crowded with moving bodies, and although at one point he and Chris find themselves lying in very close proximity, they seem quite comfortable with this. This level of concentration suggests that Santos' reading of Titania is playing out both on his 'mental stage' (Benton, 1979, p. 74) and in his physical representation, an interaction which, as Barrs (1987) proposes, allows the text to fully 'come alive' (p. 208).

In their depiction of Titania, some students test out what might be described as stereotypically effeminate movements and gestures. Meanwhile, some of the learners playing animals adopt the movements of apes or chimps in quite committed and varied ways – for example, the bow-legged walk of a chimp, loping actions, arm swinging, scratching and so on. Two boys, working together, engage in a fast and apparently hilarious chase, weaving in and out of the other bodies they encounter whilst retaining their monkey-like movements. The dual participant-spectator quality to their actions is evident in their need to simultaneously do, display and share in the pleasure. Shona is explicit with students about the degree of open-ended playfulness she expects, heightening a sense of shared discovery: 'Now this has the potential to be a lot of fun, but also kind of quite crazy [smiling], so I'm going to be quite interested to see how this works out.'

In an earlier interview, Shona expresses her belief that this type of spontaneous messiness, playfulness and physicality is closely connected with concept formation. To this end, she allows what Heathcote (2015) refers to as elaboration time for the playfulness to develop. Dramatic play has provided the springboard, but Shona next uses the music to begin the shift to a more pedagogically purposeful drama (Fleming, 2011). She now adds the rule that learners cannot touch, but they can still make sounds. The movement begins again and this time there is more focused work on creating the animals. Next Shona asks learners to channel their characterisation of an animal or fairy through movement alone with no sound effects. The deliberately chosen stately music can now be clearly heard and the effect of this is marked. Actions become dance-like and far less chaotic; some learners adopt slow motion, which not only serves to exaggerate their movements, but also allows greater precision in the execution. One boy, for instance, stands almost in the centre of the drama space absorbed in a careful mime of peeling and eating a banana, staring intently at the imagined banana whilst seemingly oblivious to the actions of the other bodies swirling around him.

Shona draws explicit attention to the value of this way of working in terms of students' learning:

Teacher: . . . What you've been really good at, many of you so far, is the playing aspect. So what we've had mmm which I think is very effective . . . What we've had that I think's been very successful is lots of . . . particularly the animals, the beasts, the creatures, lots of them very successfully playing those animals. I've seen a lot of really good work of that kind, and I've seen the beginnings of some really good work from the Titanias, though the Titanias' job is about to become much harder. So what I'm seeing so far is some good playing. Playing with Shakespeare is really important, so you're playing with the ideas. I think it's very important.

Thus she makes explicit her belief in the intellectual properties of play and the ways in which 'play for them' has connected positively with 'play for teacher'.[35] Whilst highlighting that it is 'important' for the learners to play with Shakespeare's ideas, Shona also signals that she is about to increase the level of challenge.

[35] A concept first identified by Gillham (1974) and thereafter adopted more widely amongst drama in education practitioners such as Bolton (2010) to describe this aspect of process drama pedagogy. The 'play for them' (the students) draws them in and creates their investment in the drama, but it also provides the 'children's angle of connection' (Davis, 2010, p. xvii) to the 'play for teacher'.

Shona starts the music again and now each Titania has to pair up with a beast and practise freezing in the moment when she wakes up and falls instantly in love. This signals a clear gear-change from dramatic play to 'what a child is doing when he [*sic*] is using the art form of drama' to learn 'at a subjective level of meaning' (Bolton, 1979, p. 32). It is also a pivotal moment because it connects directly to the scenes they will be reading in the following lessons. Meanwhile Shona circulates, describing the frozen scenes as they are being produced. For example, she picks out a Titania 'who is looking surprisedly but with attention at a beast', noting 'emotions of fear and unhappiness on the part of the beast'. In a second freeze-frame she remarks on a Titania who is 'reaching out, she's very interested in her pose in terms of actually getting close to this animal'; in a third, 'shock and horror whilst love and attention are coming'; and then she observes more provocatively, 'some of the animals are still quite careless; they're just doing their animal things whilst Titania is showing what she's got'. At the same time as modelling for students how to comment seriously on the work, Shona's narrative serves to draw attention to the sexual overtones of this scene.[36] Varying degrees of discomfort are apparent in some learners' body language and facial expressions, but Shona uses the tension to engage learners with the cognitive challenge of the text. This connects the dramatic play of the earlier part of the lesson with the meanings in the dramatic situations that learners construct as part of their continuing interactions with the play.

Shona asks one pair at a time to present their freeze-frame, inviting the audience of peers to 'tell me what it is you can see'. This is a way of capturing in stillness the bodiliness (Franks et al., 2014, p. 172) of the participants and the physicality of the relationships they are seeking to represent whilst allowing these aspects to be placed under scrutiny. Initially students' comments on the freeze-frames stay within the realms of what they clearly feel will be deemed acceptable by the teacher, until the gendered and sexualised undercurrents rise to the surface. Santos describes

---

[36] At the Interactive Research Conference in 1966 Heathcote and Gavin Bolton discussed the teacher's use of narration in helping students to achieve an understanding of the important features of their drama: see www.mantlenetwork.com.

Joel, frozen in his role as the beast, as 'all creeped out' and Connor follows up by saying Joel looks 'disgusted', which causes a ripple of laughter. By using Joel's name rather than referring to his animal character their comments seem personally directed, and Joel's reaction is to break his well-held freeze to give a couple of slight nods indicating his acknowledgement of his disgust. Some of the spectators go further, participating in a form of 'dark play' (Schechner, 1988, p. 12) which pushes at the boundaries of the drama in a deconstructive but not necessarily destructive manner, and this is clearly a way for them to grapple with the ambiguities of the Titania–beast relationship. Since dark play does not declare its subversion (Schechner, 1993), the spectators' comments are framed in the manner of a serious evaluation, concealing their motives by appearing to adhere to the protocols of the lesson whilst simultaneously playing with identities and what Richard Schechner calls 'alternative selves' (1988, p. 14). Thus some of the spectators take advantage of the materiality of the 'frozen' bodies under scrutiny and the depiction of the relationships between them to comment in a way that opens up the possibility for disruption of the regulatory heterosexual norms (Butler, 2011) that often exert an unspoken pressure on adolescent boys. One such example is when Isaac, who is holding a very recognisable ape-like pose, faces Ricky (as Titania) who stands with arms outstretched towards him. Both show some control in holding this pose although they cannot manage any in-role eye contact. Comments from the audience, such as Ronny suggesting that Ricky wants Isaac to go to 'his house' and that Isaac is thinking about it, instantly affect the precision of their freeze-frame by making them grin at each other in recognition of the awkwardness of this situation, until Ricky, laughing, buries his face in his hands. It is worth remembering that such comments, when taken at face value, do not stray too far from the Bottom–Titania relationship as depicted in Act 3, scene 1 and Act 4, scene 1. The students' dark play engages with the sense of sexual danger inherent in both the drama of the lesson and the play itself. It suggests that their 'real world' concerns are beginning to chime with the themes of the play, a situation Shona usefully draws on during a discussion later in the lesson.

Rather than dismissing their dark play as misbehaviour, Shona's constructive response is to provide a reflexive narrative on the freeze-frames, investing the students' learning with the meanings that have emerged from their playfulness but that they do not necessarily articulate for themselves. Her narrative lends coherence and cohesion to the action and highlights that there are different interpretative choices:

Teacher: So we're going to see a couple more [freeze-frames] in a moment. What I wanted to kind of draw your attention to before we do some more feedback – some of the feedback started to be really good – is we're starting to get some patterns here. So a lot of this idea of talking about openness, wanting to embrace, wanting to hold, the kind of trance-like stare of Titania as she magically, under the influence of magic, falls in love. And with the beast we seem to be getting two different kinds of thing, or maybe three different kinds of beast. We're getting a beast that is clearly disgusted in Joel's case, so kind of freaked out by it. We're getting a beast that is just carrying about its normal business although is a little bit surprised, perhaps in the case of Martin, but we're also getting the beast maybe in Isaac's case who actually looks quite happy and comfortable with the situation, isn't threatened by the fairy, actually quite likes the fairy's attention.

Her choice of the word 'threatened' acknowledges the reason for the discomfiture some learners have experienced during these activities. The direct nature of her 'mediation' (Moll, 1990, p. 9) in a Vygotskyan sense demonstrates what Luis Moll refers to as the 'special socialization' (p. 9) of the learners' thinking and recognises that their 'conscious awareness' of knowledge is 'primarily a product of instruction' (p. 9). However, the types of productive interaction Shona employs place 'emphasis on social activity and cultural practice as sources of thinking' (p. 15) and serve to construct a collaborative form of ZPD, a characteristic of reading through drama lessons (for an account of the ZPD of drama, see Hulson, 2006, pp. 6–7).

Shona's narrative is also a way of preparing the class for their forth-coming close study of the scenes between Bottom and Titania in the printed play script, lessons which will track the narrative and the language of the play more closely. Nevertheless, like Beth, Shona's pedagogy deliberately decentres the text, in this case by acknowledging that in this lesson there are at least three 'texts' which interact in significant ways: the script, which acts as the prompt for the learners' dramatic imaginings; the predictive text of their freeze-frame representations; and the text that is apparent in the metacommunicative signals of the learners' dark play. This last, which Shona consciously facilitates, is one they are keen to test out in a 'risky' way within the formal setting of the classroom and the curriculum.

By inviting learners' reflections on the relationships portrayed in the freeze-frames, Shona brings their counter-texts to the surface for articulation and examination. This progressively emboldens the students to take more risks in their evaluations during the final part of the lesson:

Teacher: I've got this question for you. Why – and this is not supposed to be a rhetorical question; this is a genuine question – why [in] Year 7 has this drama been so difficult to do and so difficult to talk about in a sensible way? What is it that's made the discussion and the showing quite tricky? I want to hear from you one by one [a number of learners raise their hands to offer answers].

Alexei suggests that the difficulties relate to the all-boys make-up of the class. Joel adds that their laughter and comments are caused by the fact that the drama is about love, and this links to a topic recently studied in their Personal, Health and Social Education (PHSE) sessions, which, in his words, 'makes it a bit awkward'. Although Joel does not verbalise what that topic is, all the learners are aware that they have recently been discussing sexual relationships and sexuality during PHSE. Zemar states that because the discussion is about the topic of relationships, 'people don't actually want to go into that because it's [an English lesson], not PHSE'. His use of the word 'people' deflects from the fact that they are all boys and also hints that, in speaking for others, he is speaking for himself. His compartmentalising of such discussions – suitable in PHSE but not in English – might be a tactic to avoid some issues that have taken such an uncomfortably embodied form in this lesson. Elias suggests that 'we don't want to seem all squishy and mushy', not only acknowledging the gender binary of how boys (and girls) 'perform' their 'sex' (Butler, 2011), but also the constraining nature of the 'regulatory apparatus of heterosexuality' (p. xxi). Ahmed tentatively works through some ideas about how in the fictionalised world, as in real life, there will be situations that are interpreted differently according to perspective: 'When we're like acting something out, yeah, someone might be thinking that there's something but the actor might be doing something else', and he senses that 'if you look at the language he's [Shakespeare's] using, we don't really translate it that well'. Here Ahmad gestures towards the complexities, both in and out of character, of simultaneously negotiating between the interpretations of others and the language of the script.

Shona refocuses the learners' attention on performance elements, asking them to consider the possible responses of the audiences in Shakespeare's day:

Teacher:	Having picked over what was quite difficult and tricky about what you had to do, the question I want to ask you is this. When the audience [in Shakespeare's era] see what is really a young man dressed as a fairy, Fairy Queen Titania, wake up and fall in love with another man dressed as a beast, hands up what you think the reaction is likely to be [sound of pips to signify end of lesson]?
Matty:	I'm not mmm . . . I don't know how to say it, yeah, but mmm, if I saw it, I would . . . I would say it was gay.
Teacher:	OK, so there would be issues around sexuality. How might an audience react to that? Duane?
Duane:	In some of the plays, like the people they, like, [unclear] know some of the men act in a feminine kind of way.
Teacher:	OK, so maybe some of the audience might be quite accepting of it, they'd be used to it, it wouldn't seem anything all that strange to them. I'm wondering how the audience might be reacting to Titania waking from her sleep and falling in love with this other man dressed as the beast. Joel?

Joel: People in like Shakespeare's time, yeah, 'cos women never played anyone on stage because it was all just men, and like nobody at that time would laugh. And say if like we went to a play like that and we was allowed in the old times and we had like the modern minds, we'd laugh.

Although Shona adds that 'Shakespeare's audience would laugh as well,' she has no time to pursue the discussion further as the end-of-lesson pips have sounded. However, the idea of historical distance that Shona briefly touches on is, as Yandell (2017) proposes, important in literary study, although this 'sense of pastness' (p. 596) is always bound up with the network of associations learners both bring to and encounter in the classroom. Thus the possible reactions of Shakespearean audiences to the cross-dressing ambiguities of men playing women have a direct relationship with the everyday 'performance' of sexuality in the here and now.

We are reminded here not only of Heathcote's notion of 'living through' in drama activity (see Bolton, 1998), but also of Rosenblatt's concept of 'aesthetic' and 'efferent' (Rosenblatt, 1994, p. 24) ways of reading. For Heathcote, temporarily 'living-through' (O'Neill, 2015b, p. 112) a character requires 'Thinking from *within* a situation' (p. 112). This evaluative function is important because it acts as a prompt to further learning by putting one's own responses under the spotlight so that they serve as fresh stimuli (Vygotsky, 1979). In this lesson 'what happens *during* the actual reading event' (Rosenblatt, 1994, p. 24), described by Rosenblatt as what the reader '*is living through during his* [*sic*] *relationship with that particular text*' (p. 25), occurs as part of the students' in-the-moment drama activity. Thus Heathcote's and Rosenblatt's concepts share associations with emotional and imaginative engagement, but both are also capable of evoking conscious insights into the distinction between the 'reality' of the fiction and the actuality of the 'real world'. This suggests how both types of responses are provoked when students' lived experiences connect with a significant moment in the play.

Rosenblatt's efferent stance denotes the concepts, ideas and actions that readers carry away from the text and that remain 'as the residue *after* the reading' (Rosenblatt, 1994, p. 23). Some weeks later, in a small group interview with five members of the class, the 'residue' from the students' reading through drama activity becomes clear as they are still tussling with the gender-related issues raised by this lesson:

Adam: 'Cos sometimes you might . . .
Duane: Yeah, when you have to, like you're supposed to be in love with another man.
Joel: [finger to lips, to Duane] Ssshhhh.
Adam: Yeah like say, erm . . . I don't know actually. Well, say you're acting out a girl and you don't wanna be acting out a girl. You're sort of thinking, 'well, what do I do?', and you don't know.

Having acknowledged this tension between the challenge presented by acting out the 'other' and their reluctance to engage with it, they go onto explore how such an activity might relate positively to their learning. In relation to playing female roles in English, the learners grapple with both the difficulties they perceive and the reasons for pursuing such activities:

Maggie Pitfield (MP):   When you have to do something, we're talking about something uncomfortable though, do you still see there's learning in it or not?
Duane: Yeah.
Tom: When we're girls, we're never going to learn to be girls.
                        [Joel laughs very loudly]
Duane: It's not like that. You might be acting . . .
Tom: And it's good to act out something that you wouldn't usually act out, like if you have to be like . . .
Duane: . . . you use skills of everything
Tom: Yeah, you need to learn how to . . .
Duane: . . . do stuff.
Tom: [unclear]
Duane: Emphasise. Empathise?

Duane's idea seems to encompass more than acting skills as he works his way towards the notion of empathy, and Tom's first interjection in this exchange returns once more to the question that lies at the heart of in-character activity, whether it is ever possible to learn to 'be' someone else and whether that is actually the point. Barrs (1987), Heathcote (1991), and Bolton and Heathcote (1999) would suggest not. 'For Heathcote the principal component of all acting behaviour is the "self-spectator", which protects the participants into a level of emotion from which they may remain safely detached, both *engaged* and *detached*' (Bolton, 1998, p. 200). Fleming (2019) highlights the percipient nature of drama activity, which combines 'the functions of actor and spectator that participants exercise in the immediacy of a process drama event' (Bryer, 2020, p. 87). Schechner (1985) cites the ability of both the performer and the spectator to 'believe and disbelieve at the same time' (p. 113), which creates some necessary distance 'between the character and the performer' (p. 9) into which a commentary of an ideological, aesthetic or personal nature might be inserted.

It is Joel who goes on to insert his personal commentary in the way suggested by Schechner (1985), when his learning about the play through the drama activity described earlier prompts his contemplation of a relevant real-life context:

Joel: It's like when you're older, like, say if you're acting as a girl . . . say you're thinking about LGBT[37] and stuff like that, say you're acting as a girl, like, it would basically reassure you and, like, let you basically do what's best for you, 'cos that's how my brother basically, like. found out about his personality and stuff like that, so yeah.

Duane: Your brother gay?

Joel: Yeah.

Duane: Oh, OK.

[37] Lesbian, gay, bisexual, and transgender.

Joel: Yeah. Well, he's not really my brother; he's my half-brother
            and he's older, and he's twenty-two, so, like, yeah ... I get to
            see him often.

Duane: Is it weird talking to him, well, not weird, but ... ?

Joel: It's not weird. I act like he's just normal because he doesn't seem
            it; he doesn't express it. Like the thing I don't like is people that
            really express it, I just don't like that. I like just people basically
            to be ....

Tom: Yes, it's a bit weird.
            [Both Duane and Joel adopt what they think is a very 'camp'
            posture and facial expression as a way of relieving the tension,
            whilst the others remain silent.]

Duane: He can just act, you know, he doesn't have to be over the top
            about it.

The three boys are clearly working through issues of sexuality, including
whether homosexuality means being 'like' a girl, one of the very questions
their role-play based on *MND* has raised. Thus learning *about* and *through* the
play has prompted learning *beyond* it. Joel's disclosure can be made and
discussed seriously, unaffected by face-pulling and mockery, distractions that
have surfaced at other times during the focus group conversation.

Embodying Shakespeare's Language

As we have seen, even when Beth and Shona's drama work allows learners
considerable licence to play around with ideas or situations not strictly
dictated by the play script itself, it is usually with the intention of returning
to Shakespeare's 'text' (whether in printed format or performed on film).
Nevertheless, by implication the types of approaches taken by Beth and
Shona would be criticised by John Haddon (2009) for serving to avoid the
central challenge posed by Shakespeare's language: 'Even those that involve
splendidly physical treatments of the language and awareness of theatre can
prove remarkably indifferent to questions of meaning' (p. ix). It is
a criticism we wish to contest by reference to two further examples of
observed classroom practice.

First we focus on another of Shona's *MND* lessons which examines the argument between Hermia, Helena, Demetrius and Lysander following the mistaken application of love potion to Lysander's eyes in Act 3, scene 2. Far from evading engagement with language and meaning, Shona makes a point of checking understanding of particular words and phrases as the class reads through the script. She acknowledges the insulting, sometimes racist nature of the characters' exchanges, the latter quickly spotted by this ethnically diverse group of students. (Later in the lesson Ricky returns to this aspect, speculating on the question of historical difference: 'Like, back then they must have just treated it as any other insult, but today it seems, it's more, it feels more offensive.') While providing space for students to develop their own ideas, Shona is not averse to correcting anachronistic misinterpretation where necessary, such as when Joel questions whether 'vixen' counts as an insult ('foxy' in contemporary London slang denotes sexual attractiveness). Next comes a fast-paced 'desk drama' game which requires each student to memorise one of the insults.[38] The game begins with Shona voicing the insult 'vile thing' as she points at one student; that student then points at another, saying a different insult and so on. The first time they play the game Shona asks them 'to say it in a normal voice, I don't want you to try and think too much about the meaning of the words, I want you literally just to say it'. This rendition is quite flat, but the next two rounds of the game, first shouting and then 'big stage whispering', are much more animated with students twisting in their seats eagerly following the insults as they are passed around the room. Shona then invites them to rehearse saying their insult 'in a way that you think matches its meaning best'. During this final round, two students start a game of verbal tennis, throwing the insults 'you canker-blossom' and 'You minimus of hind'ring knot-grass' back and forth between them, varying intonation and emphasis with each repetition of the insult in an attempt to increase its impact.

We note that Kate McLuskie (2009) is dismissive of this type of activity, whereby lines are 'whispered or shouted, chanted or sung' and the 'physical experience [of] vocalizing' is used to avoid addressing 'the difficult and alienating process of negotiating unfamiliar language or complex questions

---

[38] Shona excludes the racist insults from the game.

of historical difference' (p. 132). We suggest, however, that the next stage of the lesson demonstrates how playing with the language in this way can prompt students, even at this young age, to be intrigued by its unfamiliarity and to want to interrogate it further. Shona asks the students to comment freely on the meaning of the insults or anything they find interesting, and several remark on how meanings change over time. For example, Elias returns to Joel's interpretation of 'vixen' as a case in point, and then he speculates as to why 'juggler' might suggest 'cheater'. The question of historical difference also proves of interest in a discussion about the acceptability of certain words and phrases. Duane wonders whether 'dwarf' is still an appropriate term to use, and Ronny asks if 'midget', a word he has heard used more recently, is any better. In a nod towards wider conflicts in the play, Ricky highlights the tension between the theme of love and the language of abuse. The lesson moves on to a dramatic reading of Helena and Hermia's argument (3.2.195–291) performed by Shona and Ms M, the regular teaching assistant for this class, with students asked to listen as if in the role of counsellors, recording their observations and questions on special 'case notes' sheets, an activity to be continued in the following lesson. Students' attentive listening to the dramatic reading, and their spontaneous round of applause for Shona and Ms M, demonstrate their engagement and they settle quickly to completing their observation sheets before they are dismissed at the end of the lesson. As they leave the classroom some students can still be heard practising their Shakespearean insults on each other.

For our next example, we turn our attention to Marie, a recently qualified teacher in Beth's department at Eastgate School, preparing her Year 9 class (fourteen-year-olds) for their SATs test (see Section 1). As explored elsewhere (Coles, 2009), Marie's pedagogy in many ways exemplifies the tensions inherent in attempting to combine active methods with the demands of high-stakes tests. Nevertheless, in the penultimate lesson of her *Macbeth* scheme of work – and with the national test date imminent – Marie initially sets out to revise the set scenes (Act 3, scenes 1, 2 and 4) through process drama (although drama cedes ground to a more conventional worksheet-based tabulation of points and quotations in the second half of the lesson).

Marie sets up the lesson by organising the class into small groups, each given a different key quotation (one or two lines) selected by Marie from across the three scenes:

Teacher: ...The purpose of this exercise is for you to remind yourselves what happens in this scene and why that line I've given you is important, and then through your bit of drama to remind the rest of the class.

The group nearest the video camera, consisting of Liz, Zach, Tunde, Chris, Sinead and Ben, have been allocated the line 'O, full of scorpions is my mind, dear wife!' (3.2.36). At first, after leafing through copies of the play text together to locate the quotation, Tunde seems confused by the reference to scorpions ('We have to find where there are scorpions in this scene, right?') until Liz tentatively suggests they only exist in Macbeth's head. At this point Marie comes over and intervenes by prompting discussion around possible associations carried by the image of scorpions:

Tunde: They're biting him –
Liz: – stinging, poisoning him.
Teacher: Yes, imagine they are stinging him over and over again. What does that say?
Sinead: He's feeling guilty –
Liz: – can't get it out of his head. He's going mad.
Teacher [nods]: Yes, and think about what's happening between Macbeth and Lady Macbeth at this point of the play. Where are they heading? [Teacher moves on to next group.]

By the time all groups are ready to share their presentations, Liz's group have created a moving tableau: the opening freeze-frame shows Tunde (as Macbeth) and Liz (Lady Macbeth) standing facing each other, surrounded by the rest of the group, who are crouching down. Tunde clutches his head as if in anguish, then brings the tableau alive by speaking the line while Sinead, Ben, Chris and Zach rise up, closing in on Macbeth, making sibilant sounds and vicious pinching gestures with their hands; the freeze at the finish leaves Lady Macbeth on the outside of the circle looking on helplessly. Marie invites the other students to comment. One suggests it shows Macbeth 'at breaking point'; another that 'Lady Macbeth is being left out', a point Marie helps students expand with reference to the banquet scene and the broader narrative arc of the final two acts of the play. According to Haddon (2009, p. 30), activities which treat metaphors primarily as 'word pictures' are in danger of limiting interpretative possibilities. In Marie's hands, the learners' literal representation of scorpions is only the first step. She encourages students to reach beyond the visually obvious towards a deeper understanding of the complexities of Shakespeare's language within the dramatic trajectory of the play. Marie's approach, moreover, accommodates the diverse starting points of the participants and provides a Vygotskyan supportive framework for taking learning forward. In the second half of the lesson, notably, it is Tunde who volunteers an answer to Marie's whole-class question about natural imagery in the three scenes ('snakes and scorpions and crows'), which leads to a short discussion on the atmosphere created by reference to such creatures and their contribution to the sense of foreboding at this point in the play.[39]

Marie's selection of key lines to be analysed through drama is not confined to metaphors. Another group, for instance, presents the lines: 'Macbeth: Ride you this afternoon? / Banquo: Ay, my lord' (3.1.19–20). By creating an embodied form of subtext (through the use of two Macbeths), this group's dramatisation helps their audience of peers towards a grasp of dramatic irony in the ensuing whole-class reflections; and in the second half of the lesson this short exchange between Banquo and Macbeth is cross-referenced by a student to the theme of appearance and reality ('false face').

Instead of treating the text as something that needs to be heavily mediated by the teacher, Marie trusts in drama's capacity to illuminate aspects of language and imagery. She enables her Year 9 students to voice Shakespeare's words for themselves while they explore meanings in a creatively physicalised way. In contrast, we believe the privileging of the more conventional type of language study as advocated by Haddon (2009) is in danger of *disembodying* language, abstracting it from the realm

---

[39] One of the groups had presented the line 'We have scorched the snake, not killed it' (3.2.13).

of human relationships. As Stredder (2009, p. 118) asserts, 'speech and action are inextricably mixed' in normal social interaction; therefore teachers should capitalise on these interconnections, 'using actions to free words'.

5 Conclusions

Drama As an Embedded Form of Learning in English

As we have sought to establish in Section 1, Vygotsky's social constructivist understandings of knowledge formation and the important interaction between everyday and scientific concepts are crucial to our argument for drama as an embedded form of learning in English. However, it is important to note that, while we are constructing an avowedly theorised account of Shakespeare pedagogy, our proposals are irreducibly situated in real-world classroom practice. Within the limited space this Element allows, glimpses into Beth's, Shona's and Marie's English classrooms reveal them to be sites of social and cultural exchange; the ways in which their students encounter the plays of Shakespeare are central to the literary meaning-making processes that occur therein. This entails a significantly different understanding of learning than the focus on knowledge acquisition promoted by Young (2008), and so, like Doecke and Mead (2018), we refute the idea of an 'oscillating binary between knowledge and experience' (p. 253). We have therefore proposed a different model of reading Shakespeare plays, one in which 'the context of their reception' (p. 254) is as important as their historical context.

Our focus on reading Shakespeare through drama specifically draws on and finds synergies between the key concept of 'living through' in process drama (Heathcote), reading reception theory (Rosenblatt) and reading as enactment (Barrs). For Heathcote, 'living through' is a complex process dependent on the teacher's careful structuring and the students' co-creation of the drama. It enables 'a double-consciousness of immersion in the experience and self-spectatorship' (O'Neill, 2015a, p. 4) and sets up a fruitful 'inside/outside reflective dialectic' (Davis, 1998, p. xi), such as that on display in Shona's first *MND* lesson. When Rosenblatt (1994) and

Barrs (1987) apply 'living through' to literary reading, they also identify enactment as central to the process, whether as drama in the head or when physicalised through the types of activity exemplified in Section 4. As we have discussed in relation to Shona's lesson, from their different perspectives Heathcote, Rosenblatt and Barrs emphasise both the imaginative and critical demands of 'living through'. Zemar, one of the students at Woodside Boys School, neatly illustrated for us how this criticality is embedded in the drama activity of the English classroom. During an interview held shortly before his GCSE examinations he reflected on the ways in which the drama he had experienced in his English lessons – the collaborative tussling over a text, the interpretations inherent in the presentations to classmates and the subsequent interrogation of those presentations – had over time helped him to determine what he called his 'attitudes' to the texts studied.[40]

We have also drawn attention to the learning processes associated with play and its affordances when reading Shakespeare. Our analysis has led us to take issue with those criticisms which position a play-based and process drama methodology in studying a Shakespeare play as antithetical to rigorous literary engagement with a key canonical text. The manner in which Beth's students shift easily in and out of role as Henry (whether in writing or improvisation) appears to confirm Williams' (1983) and Barrs' (1987) belief in the everyday quality of role-playing. For Shona, play provides the starting point for a risky exploration of relationships and sexuality as she carefully guides (and challenges) the students towards a more in-depth understanding of a scene from *MND* until finally, because this is a script being read in an English classroom, she refocuses their attention on the performance aspects of the play. Far from abandoning their critical faculties in favour of '"pointless playing around"' (Banaji, 2011, p. 37), which is the type of criticism often levelled at these approaches, it is Beth's and Shona's pedagogical artistry that enables the students to wrestle with concepts pertinent to both the play and their own lived

---

[40] In our experience this approach works equally well in developing the degree of criticality required of A (Advanced) Level Literature students (seventeen–eighteen-year-olds).

experiences. This, surely, is the very stuff of reading – and enjoying – literature. Tellingly, enjoyment is a perspective that carries little weight as far as current policy in this area is concerned.

Teacher and Student Agency

Returning to Miriam Gilbert's (1984) observation that periodic promotions of 'active Shakespeare' seem destined to be short-lived in practice, we believe it touches on issues to do with the agency of both teachers and students. Not least in significance is the enduring policy focus on Shakespeare's status within a canon-rich curriculum and the discourse of student deficit which underpins it. We have also highlighted the danger of creating a further discourse of deficit, one which appears not to properly value English teachers' existing pedagogical and subject knowledge expertise or acknowledge day-to-day constraints on their practice. We raise questions about the ways in which major arts institutions in England and other anglophone countries have responded to the demands of curricular Shakespeare and how they have positioned their work in relation to that of English teachers. Whereas Neelands and O'Hanlon (2011) identify a daunting array of pedagogical skills as necessary for the teaching of Shakespeare (all rooted in the RSC's notion of rehearsal room pedagogy), we find their account somewhat light on the ways in which these relate to real classroom contexts. Some commentators suggest any perceived deficiencies could be remedied by training in 'drama methods' (Irish, 2008, p. 1) or acting (Schupak, 2018). The proposition that there are pedagogical gaps gives impetus to projects such as the LPN to fill them, and this is why we particularly scrutinise the sustainability of ensemble/rehearsal room practices at the classroom level (although we acknowledge that the RSC has more recently attempted to address this with its Associate Schools Programme, partnering 'Lead' Schools with a cluster of 'Associate' schools in the same geographical area).[41] We also argue in Section 2 that overly simplistic exhortations to put a Shakespeare play 'on its feet' are not grounds enough for advocating active approaches, although clearly we are not denying the power of performance. Indeed, we acknowledge the pioneering work of Gibson and O'Brien and intend that our account

---

[41] See www.rsc.org.uk/learn/associate-schools-programme; also see footnote 18.

has captured the creative spirit of the RSC and Globe's projects, albeit with the caveats outlined earlier. Nevertheless, our examples in Sections 3 and 4 reveal the complexities involved if encounters with Shakespeare are to reach beyond notions of 'access' or 'entitlement'.

If an active Shakespeare methodology is to be sustainable, it needs to be integrated into daily practice and in tune with the real contexts in which English teachers operate, as is perhaps embodied by Gibson's original project and, more recently, by the collaboratively organised, small-scale 'Shakespeare Reloaded' initiative (see Brady, 2009), or exemplified at the school level by the learning community contexts of Beth and Shona, both English curriculum leaders in their respective schools. In Section 3, for example, we identify how something as simple as relocation from a classroom to a different teaching space can signal 'special occasion' status for drama. This has repercussions for Paul and his students in terms of their perceptions of drama in relation to English, ultimately rendering his drama-based lessons unsustainable. Paul's experience exemplifies the very real challenge involved in pursuing an approach which goes against the grain of dominant discourses within and beyond his school environment. However, the types of interpretative activities that are apparent in the practices we describe in Section 4 provide a counterweight. Where teachers in our study are flexible in their use of regular classroom spaces and move fluidly across the different modes of learning in English, they demonstrate how reading Shakespeare through drama can be a sustainable pedagogical approach.

We certainly do not downplay the constraining effects of current assessment regimes on English teachers. On the contrary, we take a candid look at how this works against the use of active methods and highlight how, even for those committed to an active Shakespeare approach, professional confidence can be undermined by the dictates of narrowly defined assessment goals. Like Gibson, fundamental to our account in this Element is a respect for the professionalism of teachers and a desire to accurately reflect the ways in which they seek to shape their pedagogies to meet the interests of their students whilst fulfilling their responsibilities in terms of assessment outcomes. We recognise, for example, how Beth's practice has, by her own admission, been enriched by contact with RSC training, but we are cautious, as are Thomson et al.

(2012), about 'top-down' approaches to professional development which are not attentive to the 'complex frame of national policy, public expectations and local institutional interpretations of policy and educational purposes' within which teachers work (p. 47). Collaborative initiatives between arts organisations and schools are therefore likely to be at their most productive when they take proper account of the teachers' responsibility in 'ensuring that children meet mandated curriculum outcomes' (p. 47) and acknowledge that 'the two positions [of creative practitioners and teachers] are not the same, not interchangeable' (p. 47).

Disrupting Monocultural Hegemonic Discourses

Much of the writing for this Element was produced in the year that gave rise to a resurgence of powerful Black Lives Matter activism especially across the USA and the UK, accompanied by urgent calls to decolonise the curriculum in universities and schools. In that context it is doubly imperative that we, as white researchers, are explicit in addressing issues concerning identity and representation inevitably raised by the study of canonical literature, particularly in urban schools. Such questions unavoidably touch upon ways in which diverse readers are positioned in relation to literary texts and point towards a reconsideration of what constitutes literary knowledge, issues made more acute when the object of study is Shakespeare. Shakespeare dominates the school curriculum, not only in the UK as we described in Section 1, but also in the USA, 'the most commonly taught author in secondary classrooms' (Dyches, 2017, p. 302). Policymakers' disproportionate focus on Shakespeare and other canonical literary texts represents a narrow view of which texts are worthy of study and serves to privilege certain voices (both fictional and critical) as authoritative. As Jeanne Dyches (2018, p. 542) points out, 'canons of knowledge tell the identities, voices and histories a society values . . . but not all are . . . experienced uniformly'. It is unlikely, however, that small acts of curriculum liberalisation (e.g., the addition of texts by writers from minority backgrounds) will be sufficient in themselves to disrupt hegemonic literary discourse (see Guillory, 1993). Therefore, alongside broader curriculum reform what we are specifically proposing in this Element is a reconceptualisation of reading in the Shakespeare classroom, one which privileges students' voices and is responsive to their diverse experiences and cultural practices. As illustrated in Section 4, reading through drama is a pedagogy that acknowledges difference, and in Beth's and Shona's hands it becomes an effective means of avoiding illusory claims to Shakespeare's 'universalism' along with manufactured forms of 'relevance'. We might add that this approach could prove of interest to international Shakespeare educators mounting postcolonial critiques of new forms of globalised cultural capital (see, e.g., Kok, 2017).

In Section 3 we suggest that perceptions of Shakespeare's cultural authority need to be openly acknowledged and directly confronted in classrooms. Not only is it an issue rarely addressed in 'active Shakespeare' textbooks, we have yet to observe examples of drama-based pedagogy deal adequately with the matter of Shakespeare's monumentalism and, for us, this remains an unresolved problem. Our view is that Muna, Chaz and other students cited in Section 3 are owed the opportunity to recognise and analyse their own (sometimes negative, often confused) expectations of Shakespeare, and to unpick where these preconceptions originate from as part of the official business of the classroom. Dyches' research in urban high schools in the United States leads her to propose 'critical canon pedagogy', a direct instructional method designed to enable students to 'agently deconstruct, reconstruct and repurpose' (2018, p. 539) canonical literature. In the UK we have observed students of South Asian heritage drawing on their knowledge of popular Indian film in their analysis of *Macbeth*, deftly working across genres and cultural codes, navigating between dominant and subordinate cultural practices (see Coles, 2020). This 'process of dialogical engagement' (McLaren, 1988, p. 230) generates knowledge 'dialectically from cultural ingredients that could be – and often are – both canonical and non-canonical'. If integrated with drama-based pedagogy, we think these cases suggest productive ways forward and constitute an area for further research.

Literary Knowledge

We began Section 2 by contesting notions of reified disciplinary knowledge increasingly promoted by neoliberal administrations in the UK, the USA and Australia. The idea that canonical knowledge simply requires repackaging by teachers in order to render it deliverable (or, 'accessible') to students posits reading as a dispiritingly passive and depersonalised form of study, the sole apparent purpose of which is to memorise someone else's interpretation. As we have sought to illustrate in Section 4, close observation of classroom interactions indicates that the production of a culturally meaningful, living form of literary knowledge is rather more complex. Yandell and Brady (2016) provide a good example of this in their account of teaching *Romeo and Juliet* and the discussions it generates about familial relationships in two differently located classrooms, one just outside London, the other in Ramallah, Palestine. While not strictly arising out of drama-oriented pedagogy, it nevertheless illustrates ways in which reading experiences cannot be divorced from the social and cultural dimensions of students' lives experienced outside the classroom. Beth's teaching of *Henry V* and Shona's explorations of *MND* rest on a conception of literary culture as a living, socially situated practice rather than something preserved and inert. This is not to suggest that a knowledge base in the disciplinary field of English is unimportant, as the examples of both Beth and Shona make clear. Their skilful integration of drama with discussion, writing and reading activities, and Beth's confident multimodal mixing, capture their students' interest as well as harnessing their energies and critical powers. Subject knowledge, which continues to be forged in the crucible of classroom encounters, is central to the effectiveness of Beth's and Shona's practices. And through their role as curriculum leaders it also reaches out to a wider community of English educators.

Importantly, Beth's approach also raises very specific questions about reading and about classroom texts. Throughout this Element, we have largely followed Gibson in preferring the term 'script' (1998, p. 7) to denote the printed playtext, a lexical shift that attempts to highlight the provisional, unfinished nature of Shakespeare's dramatic works prior to enactment in one form or another. Beth takes this concept a stage further in the way she effectively decentres the printed play script through her classroom practice. Undoubtedly aided by the relative openness offered by the then current system of (circumscribed) coursework assessment, across the majority of Beth's scheme of work Branagh's film adaptation and the live re-enactments produced by students are afforded authority alongside 'the text' as objects equally worthy of interpretation and discussion. This conception of 'text' and of what it means to 'do Shakespeare' at school pushes back against the fetishisation of language and textual analysis enshrined in official policy and assessment regimes covering the period of our research and in post-2014 curriculum and assessment revisions.

Why Shakespeare?

As we intimated in earlier sections, when it comes to teaching Shakespeare we are interested as much in the 'why?' as in the 'how?', particularly within the context of curricular prescription. A question we are often asked is whether we would choose to teach Shakespeare if it were not compulsory. While we reject politicised arguments steeped in English literary exceptionalism (Shakespeare is 'the best') and take issue with the idealist myth of 'universality', we are emphatically not rejecting Shakespeare. On the contrary, we recognise that some of the very qualities that have appealed to a multitude of adaptors and filmmakers (not least, stories that imagine different visions of society, characters challenging – and abusing – authority, vivid language) offer rich material for adolescents to explore. Without doubt, students find Shakespeare hard, but interview evidence from our wider data set indicates young people often relish the challenge and the sense of achievement that brings (see Coles, 2013). Moreover, Shakespeare's very particular fusion of ideas and action lends itself perfectly to forms of collaborative, drama-based pedagogy. Williams (1985, p. 238) characterises Shakespearean drama as 'inherently multivocal', a complex notion which, it seems to us, both incorporates and reaches beyond what other commentators have variously described as Shakespeare's 'aspectuality' (Bate, 1997, p. 335), 'permissive gappiness' (Smith, 2019, p. 2) or 'provocations' (Irish, 2016, p. 71). Williams' term suggests that making meaning out of Shakespeare's plays takes place within an interconnected set of dialogical processes, both in the present and across time. This is Shakespeare's context in our context (Rosen, 2004). Capturing this paradoxical sense of 'relevance and remoteness', Gibson (1998, p. 6) draws attention to what he calls Shakespeare's 'otherness'. It is these uncertainties, accentuated by the lack of authorial voice, that facilitate the kinds of dialectical interplay between learners' own sets of everyday knowledge and curricularised Shakespeare we have observed in Beth's,

Shona's and Marie's classrooms. Indeed, Smith (2019) concludes that Shakespeare's very 'ambiguity' (p. 3) renders the plays 'wonderfully unsuited to the exam system' (p. 4), their expansive unpredictability at odds with the narrow, time-constrained rigidity of the current GCSE examination rubrics inflicted on sixteen-year-olds in England. It is a view to which we whole-heartedly subscribe for reasons which we hope our classroom observations have illustrated. It takes a particularly confident and professionally well-supported teacher – like Marie – to adopt drama-inflected approaches in the context of high-stakes testing regimes.

Another Shakespeare Is Possible

Finally, we are completing the manuscript for this Element in the midst of a global pandemic. The devastating effects of COVID-19 have not only thrown a spotlight on existing forms of structural inequality, but have also further entrenched disadvantage in the most economically and socially vulnerable communities. In the UK and elsewhere education is one of the key public services in the eye of this particular storm, with prolonged closures of schools and universities leading to unequal educational, health and emotional consequences. In such unprecedented times the systemic fault lines so clearly exposed by the crisis have provoked a grassroots re-evaluation of the pre-COVID education status quo. As restrictions are lifted, we note that psychologists and educationalists are calling for wide-ranging educational recovery programmes which place as much emphasis on creative, social and play-centred activities as on knowledge-based 'catch-up'.

At the time of writing, English and drama educators in the UK in conjunction with their professional associations are beginning to prise open fresh intellectual and professional spaces, ones which are unconstrained by policy edicts and are focused instead on alternative discourses around peda-gogy, subject knowledge acquisition and assessment. As teachers and students continue to grapple in their classrooms with the fallout from COVID, we hope pressure for change will continue to build. In terms of an inclusive, culturally responsive approach to the teaching of Shakespeare, we offer *Reading Shakespeare through Drama* as our contribution to this urgent peda-gogic debate.

References

ATL, ATM and NATE. (1998). *An Evaluation of the 1998 Key Stage 3 Tests in English and Mathematics*, London: Association of Teachers and Lecturers.

Bakhtin, M. (1981). *The Dialogic Imagination: Four Essays by M. M. Bakhtin* (C. Emerson and M. Holquist, trans.), Austin: University of Texas Press.

Ball, S. J. (1993). Education, majorism and 'the curriculum of the dead'. *Curriculum Studies*, 1(2), 195–214.

Ball, S. J. (2004). *Education for Sale! The Commodification of Everything?* Presented at the Annual Education Lecture, King's College, London.

Banaji, S. (2011). Mapping the rhetorics of creativity. In J. Sefton-Green, P. Thomson, K. Jones and L. Bresler, eds., *The Routledge International Handbook of Creative Learning*, Abingdon: Routledge, pp. 36–44.

Banks, F. (2014). *Creative Shakespeare: The Globe Education Guide to Practical Shakespeare*, London: Bloomsbury.

Barrs, M. (1987). Voice and role in reading and writing. *Language Arts*, 64(2), 8–11.

Barrs, M. (2019). Teaching bad writing. *English in Education*, 53(1), 18–31.

Bate, J. (1997). *The Genius of Shakespeare*, London: Picador.

BBC Radio 4. (2019, May 6). Start the Week with Andrew Marr: Icons of English Literature – Chaucer, Shakespeare and Dickens, London.

Benton, M. (1979). Children's responses to stories. *Children's Literature in Education*, 10(2), 68–85.

Bolton, G. (1979). *Towards a Theory of Drama in Education*, London: Longman.

Bolton, G. (1998). *Acting in Classroom Drama*, Stoke on Trent: Trentham.

Bolton, G. (2010). Towards a conceptual framework for classroom acting behaviour. In D. Davis, ed., *Gavin Bolton: Essential Writings*, Stoke on Trent: Trentham, pp. 19–44.

Bolton, G., and Heathcote, D. (1999). *So You Want to Use Role Play: A New Approach in How to Plan*, London: Trentham.

Bowell, P. (2006). The drama teacher in time plays many parts. *Drama: One Forum – Many Voices*, 13(2), 24–9.

Brady, L. (2009). 'Shakespeare Reloaded': Teacher professional development within a collaborative learning community. *Teacher Development*, 13(4), 335–48.

Bruner, J. (1986). *Actual Minds, Possible Worlds*, Cambridge, MA: Harvard University Press.

Bryer, T. (2020). 'What are the Affordances of Role in Learning through Transmedia Forms of Pedagogy?' (PhD), University College London.

Butler, J. (2011). *Bodies That Matter: On the Discursive Limits of 'Sex'*, London: Routledge Classics.

Coles, J. (1994). Enough was enough: The teachers' boycott of National Curriculum testing. *Changing English*, 1(2), 16–31.

Coles, J. (2003). Alas, poor Shakespeare: Teaching and testing at Key Stage 3. *English in Education*, 37(3), 3–12.

Coles, J. (2009). Testing Shakespeare to the limit: Teaching *Macbeth* in a Year 9 classroom. *English in Education*, 43(1), 32–49.

Coles, J. (2013). 'Every child's birthright'? Democratic entitlement and the role of canonical literature in the English National Curriculum. *Curriculum Journal*, 24(1), 50–66.

Coles, J. (2020). Wheeling out the big guns: The literary canon in the English classroom. In J. Davison and C. Daly, eds., *Debates in English Teaching*, 2nd ed., Abingdon: Routledge, pp. 103–17.

Coles, J., and Bryer, T. (2018). Reading as enactment: Transforming 'Beowulf' through drama, film and computer game. *English in Education*, 52(1), 54–66.

Colnan, S., and Semler, L. (2009). Shakespeare Reloaded (2008–10): A school and university literature research collaboration. *Australian Literary Studies for Schools*, 1, 1–17.

Cox, B. (1991). *Cox on Cox: An English Curriculum for the 1990s*, London: Hodder and Stoughton.

Daly, C. (2004). Trainee English teachers and the struggle for subject knowledge. *Changing English*, 11(1), 189–204.

Daniels, H. (1996). Introduction: Psychology in a social world. In H. Daniels, ed., *An Introduction to Vygotsky*, London: Routledge, pp. 1–27.

Daniels, H., and Downes, E. (2015). Identity and creativity: The transformative potential of drama. In S. Davis, B. Ferholt, H. Grainger-Clemson, S. M. Jansson and A. Marjanovic-Shane, eds., *Dramatic Interactions in Education: Vygotskian and Sociocultural Approaches to Drama, Education and Research*, London: Bloomsbury, pp. 97–113.

Davis, D. (1998). An appreciation of Gavin Bolton's 'Acting in Classroom Drama': By way of a foreword. In D. Davis, ed., *Acting in Classroom Drama*, Stoke on Trent: Trentham, pp. ix–xiv.

Davis, D. (ed.). (2010). *Gavin Bolton: Essential Writings*, Stoke on Trent: Trentham.

Davison, J., and Daly, C. (eds). (2019). *Learning to Teach English in the Secondary School*, London: Routledge.

DES/Welsh Office. (1989). *English for Ages 5–16 ('The Cox Report')*, London: Her Majesty's Stationery Office.

DfE. (1993). *English for Ages 5 to 16: Proposals of the Secretary of State for Education for England and Wales*, London: Her Majesty's Stationery Office.

DfE. (2014). *The National Curriculum in England: English Programmes of Study*. www.gov.uk/government/publications/national-curriculum-in-england-english-programmes-of-study

DfES. (2003). *Key Stage 3 National Strategy Drama Objectives Bank*, London: DfES Publications.

Doecke, B. (2015). Storytelling and professional learning. *Changing English*, 22(2), 142–56.

Doecke, B., and McClenaghan, D. (2011). *Confronting Practice: Classroom Investigations into Language and Learning*, Putney, NSW: Phoenix Education.

Doecke, B., and Mead, P. (2018). English and the knowledge question. *Pedagogy, Culture and Society*, 26(2), 249–64.

Dollimore, J., and Sinfield, A. (eds.). (1985). *Political Shakespeare: New Essays in Cultural Materialism*, Manchester: Manchester University Press.

Dyches, J. (2017). Shaking off Shakespeare: A white teacher, urban students, and the mediating powers of a canonical counter-curriculum. *The Urban Review*, 49(2), 300–25.

Dyches, J. (2018). Critical canon pedagogy: Applying disciplinary inquiry to cultivate canonical critical consciousness. *Harvard Educational Review*, 88(4), 538–64.

Elliott, V. (2014). The treasure house of a nation? Literary heritage, curriculum and devolution in Scotland and England in the twenty-first century. *Curriculum Journal*, 25(2), 282–300.

Evans, E. (1987). Readers recreating texts. In B. Corcoran and E. Evans, eds., *Readers, Texts, Teachers*, Portsmouth, NH: Boynton/Cook/Heinemann, pp. 22–40.

Evans, M. (1989). *Signifying Nothing: Truth's True Contexts in Shakespeare's Text*, London: Harvester Wheatsheaf.

Fleming, M. (2011). *Starting Drama Teaching*, 3rd ed., Abingdon: Routledge.

Fleming, M. (2019). *The Art of Drama Teaching*, classic ed., Abingdon: Routledge.

Fleming, M., and Stevens, D. (2015). *English Teaching in the Secondary School*, London: Routledge.

Franks, A. (1996). Drama education, the body and representation (or, the mystery of the missing bodies). *Research in Drama Education*, 1(1), 105–19.

Franks, A., Thomson, P., Hall, C. and Jones, K. (2014). Teachers, arts practice and pedagogy. *Changing English*, 21(2), 171–81.

Galloway, S., and Strand, S. (2010). *Creating a Community of Practice: Final Report to the Royal Shakespeare Company's Learning and Performance Network*, University of Warwick: CEDAR: Centre for Educational Development, Appraisal and Research.

Gibb, N. (2010). Speech to the Reform Conference. www.gov.uk/government/speeches/nick-gibb-to-the-reform-conference

Gibb, N. (2017). The Importance of Knowledge-Based Education. www.gov.uk/government/speeches/nick-gibb-the-importance-of-knowledge-based-education

Gibson, R. (ed.). (1986). *Shakespeare and Schools*, Cambridge: Cambridge Institute of Education.

Gibson, R. (ed.). (1990). *Secondary School Shakespeare*, Cambridge: Cambridge Institute of Education.

Gibson, R. (1993). 'A black day will it be to somebody'. Key Stage 3 Shakespeare. *Cambridge Journal of Education*, 23(1), 77–88.

Gibson, R. (1997). *Shakespeare's Language*, Cambridge: Cambridge University Press.

Gibson, R. (1998). *Teaching Shakespeare*, Cambridge: Cambridge University Press.

Gilbert, M. (1984). Shakespeare through performance. *Shakespeare Quarterly*, 35(5), 601–8.

Gilbert, M. (2009). A test of character. In G. B. Shand, ed., *Teaching Shakespeare: Passing It On*, Chichester: Wiley-Blackwell, pp. 91–104.

Gillham, G. (1974). Report on Condercum School Project (unpublished), Newcastle Upon Tyne LEA.

Giovanelli, M., and Mason, J. (2018). Reading, readers and English: Editors' introduction. *English in Education*, 52(1), 2–4.

Gove, M. (2010). Speech to the Conservative Party Conference. https://conservative-speeches.sayit.mysociety.org/speech/601441

Guillory, J. (1993). *Cultural Capital: The Problem of Literary Canon Formation*, Chicago: University of Chicago Press.

Haddon, J. (2009). *Teaching Reading Shakespeare*, Abingdon: Routledge.

Harvey, D. (2005). *A Brief History of Neo-liberalism*, Oxford: Oxford University Press.

Haughey, J. (2012). 'What's past is prologue': 'English Journal' roots of a performance-based approach to teaching Shakespeare. *English Journal*, 101(3), 60–65.

Heathcote, D. (1980). *Drama As Context*, Sheffield: National Association for the Teaching of English.

Heathcote, D. (1991). Role-taking. In L. Johnson and C. O'Neill, eds., *Dorothy Heathcote: Collected Writing on Education and Drama*, Evanston, IL: Northwestern University Press, pp. 49–53.

Heathcote, D. (2015). Thresholds of security. In C. O'Neill, ed., *Dorothy Heathcote on Education and Drama: Essential Writings*, Abingdon: Routledge, pp. 18–22.

Hirsch, E. (1987). *Cultural Literacy: What Every American Needs to Know*, Boston: Houghton Mifflin.

Hirsch, E. (2007). *The Knowledge Deficit: Closing the Shocking Educational Gap for American Children*, Boston: Houghton Mifflin.

Holderness, G. (2014). 'Thirty Year Ago': The complex legacy of political shakespeare. Shakespeare Association of America, St Louis. https://uhra.herts.ac.uk/bitstream/handle/2299/15830/6_Holderness.pdf?sequence=4

Holzman, L. (2010). Without creating ZPDs there is no creativity. In M. C. Connery, V. John-Steiner and A. Marjanovic-Shane, eds.,

Vygotsky and Creativity: A Cultural-historical Approach to Play, Meaning Making and the Arts, New York: Peter Lang, pp. 27–39.

Hornbrook, D. (1988). 'Go play, boy, play': Shakespeare and educational drama. In G. Holderness, ed., *The Shakespeare Myth*, Manchester: Manchester University Press, pp. 145–159.

Hudson, A. K. (1954). *Shakespeare and the Classroom*, London: William Heinemann.

Hulson, M. (2006). *Schemes for Classroom Drama*, Stoke on Trent: Trentham.

Irish, T. (2008). *Teaching Shakespeare: A History of the Teaching of Shakespeare in England.* https://cdn2.rsc.org.uk/sitefinity/education-pdfs/articles-and-reports/rsc-education-history-of-teaching-shakespeare.pdf?sfvrsn=e5025b21_2

Irish, T. (2011). Would you risk it for Shakespeare? A case study of using active approaches in the English classroom. *English in Education*, 45(1), 6–19.

Irish, T. (2016). 'Possible Shakespeares: The Educational Value of Working with Shakespeare through Theatre-based Practice' (PhD), University of Warwick. http://webcat.warwick.ac.uk/record=b3111834~S15

Iser, W. (1978). *The Act of Reading: A Theory of Aesthetic Response*, London: Routledge and Kegan Paul.

Iser, W. (1989). *Prospecting: From Reader Response to Literary Anthropology*, Baltimore, MD: Johns Hopkins University Press.

Jackson, A. (2007). *Theatre, Education and the Making of Meanings: Art or Instrument?* Manchester: Manchester University Press.

Jewitt, C., and Jones, K. (2008). Multimodal discourse analysis: The case of 'ability' in UK secondary school English. In V. K. Bhatia, J. Flowerdew, and R. H. Jones, eds., *Advances in Discourse Studies*, Oxon: Routledge, pp. 149–160.

Johnson, L., and O'Neill, C. (eds.). (1991). *Dorothy Heathcote: Collected Writings on Education and Drama*, Evanston, IL: Northwestern University Press.

Jones, K. (ed.). (1992). *English and the National Curriculum: Cox's Revolution?* London: Kogan Page in association with the Institute of Education, University of London.

Jones, K. (2003). Culture reinvented as management: English in the new urban school. *Changing English*, 10(2), 143–53.

Jones, K. (2016). *Education in Britain: 1944 to the Present*, 2nd ed., Cambridge: Polity Press.

Kok, S. M. (2017). 'What's past is prologue': Post-colonialism, globalisation, and the demystification of Shakespeare in Malaysia. *SARE: Southeast Asian Review of English*, 54(1), 36–52.

Kress, G. R., Jewitt, C., Bourne, J. et al. (2005). *English in Urban Classrooms: A Multimodal Perspective on Teaching and Learning*, London: RoutledgeFalmer.

Lester, J. A. (1926). The active English class: A visit to Caldwell Cook's 'Mummery' at the Perse School, in Cambridge, England. *The English Journal*, 15(6), 443–9.

Lindsay, G., Winston, J., Franks, A., and Lees, D. (2018). *The Work of Royal Shakespeare Company Education in the First Year of the Associate Schools Programme*, Warwick:Centre for Educational Development, Appraisal and Research.

LoMonico, M. (2009). Shakespearean ruminations and innovations. *English Journal*, 99(1), 21–8.

Mackaness, G. (1928). *Inspirational Teaching*, London: Dent.

McLaren, P. (1988). Culture or canon? Critical pedagogy and the politics of literacy. *Harvard Educational Review*, 58(2), 213–34.

McLuskie, K. (2009). Dancing and thinking: Teaching 'Shakespeare' in the twenty-first century. In G. B. Shand, ed., *Teaching Shakespeare: Passing It On*, Chichester: Blackwell, pp. 123–41.

Miller, J. (1995). Trick or treat? The autobiography of the question. *English Quarterly*, 27(3), 22–6.

Moll, L. C. (1990). Introduction. In L. C. Moll, ed., *Vygotsky and Education: Instructional Implications and Applications of Sociohistorical Psychology*, Cambridge: Cambridge University Press, pp. 1–28.

Montgomerie, D., and Ferguson, J. (1999). Bears don't need phonics: An examination of the role of drama in laying the foundations for critical thinking in the reading process. *Research in Drama Education*, 4(1), 11–20.

Neelands, J. (2008). Common culture: Diversity and power in English/drama/media classrooms. *English Drama Media*, 11, 9–15.

Neelands, J. (2009). Acting together: Ensemble as a democratic process in art and life. *Research in Drama Education*, 14(2), 173–89.

Neelands, J. (2010). The meaning of drama. In P. O'Connor, ed., *Creating Democratic Citizenship through Drama Education: The Writings of Jonothan Neelands*, London: Trentham, pp. 67–78.

Neelands, J., and Goode, T. (2000). *Structuring Drama Work: A Handbook of Available Forms in Theatre and Drama*, 2nd ed., Cambridge: Cambridge University Press.

Neelands, J., and O'Hanlon, J. (2011). There is some soul of good: An action-centred approach to teaching Shakespeare in schools. In P. Holland, ed., *Shakespeare Survey 64*, Cambridge: Cambridge University Press, pp. 240–50.

Newbolt, H. (1921). *The Teaching of English in England ('The Newbolt Report')*, London: His Majesty's Stationery Office.

O'Brien, P. (ed.). (1993). *Shakespeare Set Free: Teaching* Romeo and Juliet, Macbeth, A Midsummer Night's Dream, New York: Washington Square Press.

O'Brien, P. (2009). What's past . . . *English Journal*, 99(1), 29–30.

O'Brien, P. (2019). The Folger Method: The what and how of teaching any literature. https://teachingshakespeareblog.folger.edu/2019/10/18/folger-method-eight-principles

O'Connor, P. (ed.). (2010). *Creating Democratic Citizenship through Drama Education: The Writings of Jonothan Neelands*, London: Trentham.

Olive, S. (2015). *Shakespeare Valued: Education Policy and Pedagogy 1989–2009*, Bristol: Intellect.

O'Neill, C. (2015a). Introduction. In C. O'Neill, ed., *Dorothy Heathcote on Education and Drama: Essential Writings*, Abingdon: Routledge, pp. 1–7.

O'Neill, C. (2015b). Part III Mantle of the Expert: Introduction. In C. O'Neill, ed., *Dorothy Heathcote on Education and Drama: Essential Writings*, Abingdon: Routledge, pp. 37–41.

O'Neill, C., Lambert, A., Linnell, R., and Warr-Wood, J. (1976). *Drama Guidelines*, London: Heinemann Educational Books/London Drama.

O'Neill, C., and Rogers, T. (1994). Drama and literary response: Prying open the text. *English in Australia*, (108), 47–51.

Pitfield, M. (2006). Making a crisis out of a drama: The relationship between English and drama within the English curriculum for ages 11–14. *Changing English*, 13(1), 97–109.

Pitfield, M. (2013). The impact of curriculum hierarchies on the development of professional self in teaching: Student teachers of drama negotiating issues of subject status at the interface between drama and English. *Pedagogy, Culture and Society*, 21(3), 403–26.

Pitfield, M. (2020). 'Reading through Drama: The Contribution That Drama Makes to Teaching and Learning in English' (PhD), University of Nottingham.

Qualifications and Curriculum Authority (2007). *The National Curriculum 2007*, London: Qualifications and Curriculum Authority.

Qualifications and Curriculum Authority (2002). *Standards at Key Stage 3: English*, London: Qualifications and Curriculum Authority.

Rosen, H. (2017). The democratic mode. In J. Richmond, ed., *Harold Rosen: Writings on Life, Language and Learning 1958 to 2008*. London: UCL Institute of Education Press, pp. 314–29.

Rosen, M. (2004). *William Shakespeare: In His Times, for Our Times*, London: Redwords.

Rosenblatt, L. (1994). *The Reader, the Text, the Poem: The Transactional Theory of the Literary Work*, Carbondale: Southern Illinois University Press.

Royal Shakespeare Company (2016). *The Learning and Performance Network: Final Impact Report 2016*, Stratford: Royal Shakespear Company. https://cdn2.rsc.org.uk/sitefinity/education-pdfs/lpn-10-years-of-transforming-experiences-of-shakespeare/the-learning-and-performance-network-final-impact-evaluation-report-2016.pdf?sfvrsn=e3b42921_2

Schechner, R. (1985). *Between Theater and Anthropology*, Philadelphia: University of Pennsylvania Press.

Schechner, R. (1988). Playing. *Play and Culture*, 1, 3–9.

Schechner, R. (1993). *The Future of Ritual*, London: Routledge.

Schupak, E. B. (2018). Shakespeare and performance pedagogy: Overcoming the challenges. *Changing English*, 25(2), 163–79.

Sinfield, A. (2004). *Literature, Politics and Culture in Postwar Britain*, London: Continuum.

Smith, E. (2019). *This Is Shakespeare*, London: Pelican.

Stredder, J. (2009). *The North Face of Shakespeare: Activities for Teaching the Plays*, Cambridge: Cambridge University Press.

Swain, J. (2006). An ethnographic approach to researching children in junior school. *International Journal of Social Research Methodology*, 9(3), 199–213.

The English Association. (1908). *The Teaching of Shakespeare in Schools*, Oxford: The English Association.

Thomson, P., Hall, C., Jones, K., and Sefton-Green, J. (2012). *The Signature Pedagogies Project: Final Report*, Creativity, Culture and Education. www.creativitycultureeducation.org//wp-content/uploads/2018/10/Signature_Pedagogies_Final_Report_April_2012.pdf

Thomson, P., Hall, C., Thomas, D., Jones, K., and Franks, A. (2010). *A Study of the Learning and Performance Network: An Education Programme of the Royal Shakespeare Company*, Newcastle: Creativity, Culture and Education.

Trivedi, P. (2011). 'You taught me language': Shakespeare in India. In P. Holland, ed., *Shakespeare Survey: Volume 64: Shakespeare As Cultural Catalyst*, Cambridge: Cambridge University Press, pp. 231–9.

Vygotsky, L. S. (1931). Imagination and creativity of the adolescent. www.marxists.org/archive/vygotsky/works/1931/adolescent/ch12.htm

Vygotsky, L. S. (1933). Play and its role in the mental development of the child. www.marxists.org/archive/vygotsky/works/1933/play.htm

Vygotsky, L. S. (1978). *Mind in Society: The Development of Higher Psychological Processes*, Cambridge, MA: Harvard University Press.

Vygotsky, L. S. (1979). Consciousness as a problem of psychology of behaviour. *Soviet Psychology*, 17, 5–35.

Vygotsky, L. S. (1986). *Thought and Language*, Cambridge, MA: MIT Press.

Vygotsky, L. S. (2004). Imagination and creativity in childhood. *Journal of Russian and East European Psychology*, 42(1), 7–97.

Williams, R. (1977). *Marxism and Literature*, Oxford: Oxford University Press.

Williams, R. (1983). Drama in a dramatized society. In *Writing in Society*, London: Verso, pp. 11–21.

Williams, R. (1985). Afterword. In J. Dollimore and A. Sinfield, *Political Shakespeare: New Essays in Cultural Materialism*, Manchester: Manchester University Press, pp. 231–9.

Winston, J. (2015). *Transforming the Teaching of Shakespeare with the Royal Shakespeare Company*, London: Bloomsbury Arden Shakespeare.

Wood, D. J., Bruner, J. S., and Ross, G. (1976). The role of tutoring in problem solving. *Journal of Child Psychology and Psychiatry*, 17(2), 89–100.

Yandell, J. (1997). Reading Shakespeare, or Ways with Will. *Changing English*, 4(2), 277–94.

Yandell, J. (2016). *The Social Construction of Meaning: Reading Literature in Urban English Classrooms*, London: Routledge.

Yandell, J. (2017). Knowledge, English and the formation of teachers. *Pedagogy, Culture and Society*, 25(4), 583–99.

Yandell, J. (2019). English teachers and research: Becoming our own experts. *Changing English*, 26(4), 430–41.

Yandell, J., and Brady, M. (2016). English and the politics of knowledge. *English in Education*, 50(1), 44–59.

Yandell, J., Coles, J., and Bryer, T. (2020). Shakespeare for all? Some reflections on the Globe Theatre's Playing Shakespeare with Deutsche Bank project. *Changing English*, 27(2), 208–28.

Young, M. (2008). *Bringing Knowledge Back In: From Social Contructivism to Social Realism in the Sociology of Education*, London: Routledge.

Cambridge Elements ⁼

Elements in Shakespeare and Pedagogy

Liam E. Semler
University of Sydney

Liam E. Semler is Professor of Early Modern Literature in the
Department of English at the University of Sydney. He is author
of *Teaching Shakespeare and Marlowe: Learning versus the System*
(2013) and co-editor (with Kate Flaherty and Penny Gay) of
Teaching Shakespeare beyond the Centre: Australasian Perspectives
(2013). He is editor of *Coriolanus: A Critical Reader* (2021) and
co-editor (with Claire Hansen and Jackie Manuel) of
*Reimagining Shakespeare Education: Teaching and Learning
through Collaboration* (Cambridge, forthcoming). His most recent
book outside Shakespeare studies is *The Early Modern Grotesque:
English Sources and Documents 1500–1700* (2019). Liam leads the
Better Strangers project which hosts the open-access
Shakespeare Reloaded website (shakespearereloaded.edu.au).

Gillian Woods
Birkbeck College, University of London

Gillian Woods is Reader in Renaissance Literature and Theatre
at Birkbeck College, University of London. She is the author of
Shakespeare's Unreformed Fictions (2013; joint winner of
Shakespeare's Globe Book Award), *Romeo and Juliet:
A Reader's Guide to Essential Criticism* (2012), and numerous
articles about Renaissance drama. She is the co-editor (with
Sarah Dustagheer) of *Stage Directions and Shakespearean
Theatre* (2018). She is currently working on a new edition of
A Midsummer Night's Dream for Cambridge University Press,

as well as a Leverhulme-funded monograph about Renaissance theatricalities. As founding director of the Shakespeare Teachers' Conversations, she runs a seminar series that brings together university academics, schoolteachers and educationalists from non-traditional sectors, and she regularly runs workshops for schools.

ABOUT THE SERIES

The teaching and learning of Shakespeare around the world is complex and changing. *Elements in Shakespeare and Pedagogy* synthesises theory and practice, including provocative, original pieces of research, as well as dynamic, practical engagements with learning contexts.

Cambridge Elements

Elements in Shakespeare and Pedagogy

ELEMENTS IN THE SERIES

Shakespeare and Virtual Reality
Edited by Stephen Wittek and David McInnis

Reading Shakespeare through Drama
Jane Coles and Maggie Pitfield

A full series listing is available at: www.cambridge.org/ESPG